Readings in Literary Criticism 20

CRITICS ON EMERSON

Readings in Literary Criticism

1. CRITICS ON KEATS
2. CRITICS ON CHARLOTTE AND EMILY BRONTË
3. CRITICS ON POPE
4. CRITICS ON MARLOWE
5. CRITICS ON JANE AUSTEN
6. CRITICS ON CHAUCER
7. CRITICS ON BLAKE
8. CRITICS ON VIRGINIA WOOLF
9. CRITICS ON D. H. LAWRENCE
10. CRITICS ON YEATS
11. CRITICS ON DRYDEN
12. CRITICS ON MELVILLE
13. CRITICS ON WHITMAN
14. CRITICS ON EMILY DICKINSON
15. CRITICS ON EZRA POUND
16. CRITICS ON HAWTHORNE
17. CRITICS ON ROBERT LOWELL
18. CRITICS ON HENRY JAMES
19. CRITICS ON WALLACE STEVENS
20. CRITICS ON EMERSON
21. CRITICS ON MARK TWAIN
22. CRITICS ON POE

CRITICS ON EMERSON

Readings in Literary Criticism

Edited by Thomas J. Rountree

University of Miami Press
Coral Gables, Florida

This anthology © 1973 by University of Miami Press

Manufactured in the United States of America

Library of Congress Cataloging in Publication Data

Rountree, Thomas J   comp.
    Critics on Emerson.

    (Readings in literary criticism, 20)
    Bibliography: p.
    1. Emerson, Ralph Waldo, 1803-1882. I. Title.
PS1638.R6   814'.3   73-77552
ISBN 0-87024-237-7

CONTENTS

ACKNOWLEDGMENTS   7
INTRODUCTION   9
TABLE OF IMPORTANT DATES   11

CONTEMPORARY RESPONSES   13

Thomas Carlyle, Francis Bowen, Samuel Osgood,
Orestes Augustus Brownson, C. C. Felton, C. A. Bartol,
C. E. Norton, *The North American Review,* James
Russell Lowell

NINETEENTH-CENTURY PERSPECTIVES   44

Theodore Parker, Henry James, Jr., Matthew Arnold,
Oliver Wendell Holmes, Edmund Clarence Stedman,
Charles J. Woodbury, John Jay Chapman, Thomas
Wentworth Higginson

TWENTIETH-CENTURY CRITICAL ESSAYS

ROBERT LEE FRANCIS
The Architectonics of Emerson's *Nature*   70

KENNETH BURKE
I, Eye, Ay—Emerson's Early Essay on "Nature"   74

JOEL PORTE
Nature as Symbol: Emerson's Noble Doubt   79

HENRY NASH SMITH
Emerson's Problem of Vocation: A Note on "The
    American Scholar"   82

GEORGE EDWARD WOODBERRY
Emerson's "Divinity School Address"   84

STUART C. WOODRUFF
Emerson's "Self-Reliance" and "Experience": A
    Comparison   87

ROBERT DETWEILER
The Over-Rated "Over-Soul"   91

WALTER BLAIR and CLARENCE FAUST
Emerson's Literary Method—the Essay "Art"   94

6 CONTENTS

F. O. MATTHIESSEN
The Democratic Core of *Representative Men*   100

FREDERIC IVES CARPENTER
Orientalism in *The Conduct of Life*   103

SEYMOUR L. GROSS
Emerson and Poetry   104

RICHARD P. ADAMS
Emerson and the Organic Metaphor   112

NEWTON ARVIN
The House of Pain: Emerson and the Tragic Sense   121

SELECTED BIBLIOGRAPHY   127

ACKNOWLEDGMENTS

Richard P. Adams: reprinted by permission of the Modern Language Association of America from "Emerson and the Organic Metaphor," *PMLA*, Vol. 69 (March 1954), 117-30.

Newton Arvin: from "The House of Pain: Emerson and the Tragic Sense." Reprinted by permission from *The Hudson Review*, Vol. 12, No. 1 (Spring 1959). Copyright © 1959 by The Hudson Review, Inc.

Walter Blair and Clarence Faust: from "Emerson's Literary Method," *Modern Philology*, Vol. 42 (Nov. 1944), published by the University of Chicago Press and reprinted by permission of Walter Blair and The University of Chicago Press.

Kenneth Burke: originally published in *The Sewanee Review*, Vol. 74 (Autumn 1966), the essay "I, Eye, Ay—Emerson's Early Essay on 'Nature' " appears as chapter six in *Language as Symbolic Action* by Kenneth Burke, published by The University of California Press; reprinted by permission of *The Sewanee Review* and The Regents of the University of California.

Frederic Ives Carpenter: from *Emerson and Asia* published by Harvard University Press. Reprinted by permission of the publisher.

Robert Detweiler: from "The Over-Rated 'Over-Soul,' " *American Literature*, Vol. 36 (March 1964), 65, 66-68. Copyright 1964 by the Duke University Press. Reprinted by permission of the publisher.

Robert Lee Francis: from "The Architectonics of Emerson's *Nature*," *American Quarterly*, Vol. 19, No. 1 (Spring 1967). Copyright, 1967, Trustees of the University of Pennsylvania. Reprinted by permission of the publisher.

Seymour L. Gross: from "Emerson and Poetry," *The South Atlantic Quarterly*, Vol. 54 (Jan. 1955). Copyright 1955 by the Duke University Press. Reprinted by permission of the publisher.

F. O. Matthiessen: excerpts from *American Renaissance: Art and Expression in the Age of Emerson and Whitman*, copyright 1941 by Oxford University Press, Inc. Reprinted by permission.

Joel Porte: from "Nature as Symbol: Emerson's Noble Doubt," *The New England Quarterly*, Vol. 37 (Dec. 1964), 462-76. Reprinted by permission of the author and the publisher.

Henry Nash Smith: from "Emerson's Problem of Vocation: A Note on 'The American Scholar,' " *The New England Quarterly*, Vol. 12 (March 1939). Reprinted by permission of the publisher.

Stuart C. Woodruff: from "Emerson's 'Self-Reliance' and 'Experience': A Comparison," *The Emerson Society Quarterly*, No. 47 (1967). Reprinted by permission of the Emerson Society.

INTRODUCTION

WHEN IN "The American Scholar" Ralph Waldo Emerson stressed "creative reading as well as creative writing," he may well have set the pattern for many of his future critics with the statement that "One must be an inventor to read well." He believed that what a reader derived from a book depended largely on what experience and knowledge he brought to the book. Hence when a critic of Emerson's writings sometimes reflects, or appears to reflect, as much or more of his own time and thought than that of Emerson, readers of the critics need to note the fact without being alarmed. From his vantage point of nineteenth-century idealistic trust in the oneness of man and of truth, Emerson would calmly have said to the critic as in *Nature* he said to the "kingdom of man" in general: "Build therefore your own world."

From the time of Emerson's first publications, some critics appear to have done just that, while different ones carefully and sympathetically endeavored to evaluate and clarify all or part of Emerson's world itself. Some of the early reviewers used their reviews as an opportunity to voice their own concepts rather than describe Emerson's works critically. Others varied. In *The North American Review* for April 1847 an anonymous critic ridiculed Emerson's *Poems* and attacked Emerson as a corrupter of taste who "is a chartered libertine," a writer of "enigmas both in prose and verse." On the other hand, in *The New Englander* for November 1856 N. Porter, Jr., called Emerson "an inveterate humorist" and spoke approvingly of *English Traits* as Emerson's best volume. Among the better reasoned and admiring contemporary criticisms, however, three "omissions" were frequently noted: a lack of specific, functional application of Emerson's "airy" theories; his "failure" to put his theories into a system; and the lack of Christian religious content of a fideistic nature. In his letters from England, even Carlyle salted his genuine praise with a recurring demurral.

More and more in the nineteenth century Emerson came to be looked upon as an exemplary person whose influence was to be sought in both his lectures and his published works. In 1850 Theodore Parker wrote one of the first of the summary estimates that, right up to Josephine Miles's of the present time, have served Emerson's fame. Perhaps the most influential single essay was the one wherein, almost nine decades ago, Matthew Arnold lauded Emerson as "the friend and aider of those who would live in the spirit" but denied him greatness as a writer or philosopher.

Later criticism has done much to compensate for Arnold's denial, but not without debate in some quarters. Yvor Winters has called Emerson "a fraud and a sentimentalist," and Seymour L. Gross's essay illustrates the negative reaction that Emerson's poetry can still elicit. T. S. Eliot and others, charging that the Concord transcendentalist lacked "the vision of Evil," brought about the defense by Newton Arvin. John Jay Chapman and F. O. Matthiessen are among those who emphasize Emerson's importance for the development of American democracy. Richard P. Adams examines his philosophy of organicism, while others have stressed his anticipation of the pragmatists and the modern philosophers of symbolism. Walter Blair and Clarence Faust explore his aesthetics, as Vivian C. Hopkins was also to do in her later book. And one critic has ventured into a rather wordy elucidation of Emerson's concept of the soul because we appear today to have lost that meaning.

The times seem to need critical clarification of Emerson the man and writer—clarification that is being met, as I hope this present collection of edited essays will indicate. It has been my object to represent, as fully as the limits of this book will allow, both the variety of critical approaches to Emerson's work and the temporal development of that criticism. The first two sections of the book present early responses and perspectives in their chronological order, but thereafter in section three the student of temporal critical development can check the dates of the essays and read them in their historical progression. Sections two and three are designed first for the reader who will want to move from the general to the more specific. Thus I have tried to arrange for the beginning student of criticism to have two major procedures available to him, while at the same time I feel that I have included works which the specialist will want to read if they are new to him or will want to reread if (as most will doubtless be) they are familiar. In addition, in the selected bibliography, I have given "reprint" information on valuable editions and critical books that have been long out of print.

Because of the conflict between the page limitations of the book and my desire to be as representatively inclusive as possible of the extensive body of Emerson criticism, I have made every effort to keep the essence in tone and content of the full essays herein represented. In some instances, however, the reader may want to seek the original printings for valuable extensions such as Kenneth Burke's further comparison and contrast of tragedy and transcendentalism. The good reader, of course, will also want to go on to other criticisms, while the best reader will do that and then turn back to Emerson's poems and essays.

If this book is instrumental to that result for the best reader, then it will have justified itself, I think, in regard to the worlds "built" by the critics and by Emerson. For today's "creative" reader the two are hardly separable.

University of South Alabama, 1973   THOMAS J. ROUNTREE

TABLE OF IMPORTANT DATES

1803	Born May 25 in Boston, Massachusetts, the fourth child of the Reverend William and Ruth Emerson.
1811	His father died (May 12).
1812-1817	Attended the Boston Latin School.
1817-1821	Attended Harvard College. Began keeping journals.
1821-1825	Taught school.
1825	His older brother William returned from Germany, bringing news of Goethe and of the new biblical criticism.
1825-1826	Studied divinity at Harvard and occasionally taught school.
1826	First read Coleridge. Approbated to preach as a Unitarian minister (October 10). Threatened with tuberculosis. Sailed for Charleston and Saint Augustine.
1828	Temporary insanity of his brother Edward.
1829	Ordained pastor of Second Church, Boston (March 11). Married Ellen Louisa Tucker (September 30).
1829-1831	Renewed reading in Coleridge.
1831	Ellen died (February 8).
1832	Resignation from Second Church accepted (October 28). Sailed for Europe in December.
1833	Traveled in Italy, France, and Britain. Visited Carlyle at Craigenputtock (August 25) and also met Coleridge and Wordsworth.
1834	His brother Edward died (October 10). Preached occasionally and began first series of lectures. Moved to Concord, Massachusetts.
1835	Gave lectures on *Biography*. Met Bronson Alcott and Margaret Fuller. Married Lydia Jackson (September 14).
1835-1836	Gave lectures on *English Literature*.
1836	Met Henry David Thoreau. Emerson's brother Charles died (May 9). Published *Nature* (September 9). His first child Waldo was born (October 30).
1836-1837	Gave lectures on *The Philosophy of History*.
1837	Delivered the Phi Beta Kappa address on "The American Scholar" at Cambridge, Massachusetts (August 31).
1837-1838	Gave lectures on *Human Culture*.
1838	Delivered the "Divinity School Address" at Cambridge (July 15).
1838-1839	Gave lectures on *Human Life*.
1839	His first daughter Ellen was born (February 24).

1839-1840   Gave lectures on *The Present Age.*

1840   *The Dial* first published, including Emerson's "Address to the Reader."

1841   Published *Essays, First Series* (March 20). His second daughter Edith was born (November 22). Brook Farm was founded.

1841-1842   Gave lectures on *The Times.*

1842   His son Waldo died (January 27). Met Horace Greeley and Henry James, Sr. Assumed editorship of *The Dial* in July. Hawthorne moved to Concord.

1844   His son Edward was born (July 10). Published *Essays, Second Series* (October 19).

1845-1846   Gave lectures on *Representative Men.*

1846   Published *Poems* (December 25, but dated as 1847).

1847-1848   Made his second trip to Britain and Europe. Visited Carlyle again in London. Lectured in England and Scotland.

1849   Published *Nature; Addresses and Lectures* in September and *Representative Men* in December (but dated as 1850).

1850   Made his first journey west to Saint Louis and Chicago. Margaret Fuller Ossoli died (July 19).

1851   Gave lectures on *The Conduct of Life.*

1852   Edited *Memoirs of Margaret Fuller Ossoli.*

1853   Lectured through the West.

1855   In December met Walt Whitman, author of *Leaves of Grass* (published July 4, 1855).

1856   Published *English Traits* (August 6).

1857   "Days" and "Brahma" published in first issue of *The Atlantic Monthly.*

1860   Published *The Conduct of Life* (December 8).

1862   Lectured in Washington, D.C., and met Abraham Lincoln. Thoreau died (May 6) and Emerson gave the funeral address.

1863   Celebrated the Emancipation Proclamation with "The Boston Hymn."

1866   Received LL.D. from Harvard.

1867   Lectured to St. Louis Philosophical Society. Published *May-Day and Other Pieces* (April 28). Elected overseer of Harvard.

1870   Published *Society and Solitude* in March. Gave course of fourteen lectures at Harvard.

1871   Traveled to California.

1872   His house burned (July 24).

1872-1873   Journeyed to Near East, Europe, and Britain. Made third visit with Carlyle.

1882   Died April 27 at Concord.

Contemporary Responses

THOMAS CARLYLE (Letters to Emerson)

5 Cheyne Row, Chelsea, London,
13 February, 1837.

YOUR LITTLE azure-colored *Nature* gave me true satisfaction. I read it, and then lent it about to all my acquaintance that had a sense for such things; from whom a similar verdict always came back. You say it is the first chapter of something greater. I call it rather the Foundation and Ground-plan on which you may build whatsoever great and true has been given you to build. It is the true Apocalypse, this when the "Open Secret" becomes revealed to a man. I rejoice much in the glad serenity of soul with which you look out on this wondrous Dwelling-place of yours and mine,—with an ear for the *Ewigen Melodien*, which pipe in the winds round us, and utter themselves forth in all sounds and sights and things: *not* to be written down by gamut-machinery; but which all right writing is a kind of attempt to write down. You will see what the years will bring you. It is not one of your smallest qualities in my mind, that you *can* wait so quietly and let the years do their hest. He that cannot keep himself quiet is of a morbid nature; and the thing he yields us will be like him in that, whatever else it be.

Miss [Harriet] Martineau (for I have seen her since I wrote) tells me you "are the only man in America" who has quietly set himself down on a competency to follow his own path, and do the work his own will prescribes for him. Pity that you were the only one! But be one, nevertheless; be the first, and there will come a second and a third. . . .

Chelsea, London, 8 December, 1837.

And so now by a direct transition I am got to the *Oration* ["The American Scholar"]. My friend! you know not what you have done for me there. It was long decades of years that I had heard nothing but the infinite jangling and jabbering, and inarticulate twittering and screeching, and my soul had sunk down sorrowful, and said there is no articulate speaking then any more, and thou art solitary among stranger-creatures? and lo, out of the West comes a clear utterance, clearly recognizable as a *man's* voice, and I *have* a kinsman and brother: God be thanked for it! I could have *wept* to read that speech; the clear high melody of it went tingling through my heart; I said to my wife, "There, woman!" She read; and returned, and charges me to return for answer, "that there had been nothing met with like it since Schiller went silent." My brave Emerson! And all this has been lying silent, quite tranquil in him, these seven years, and the "vociferous platitude" dinning his ears on all sides, and he quietly answering no word; and a whole world of Thought has silently built itself in these calm depths, and, the day being come, says quite softly, as if it were a common thing, "Yes, I *am* here too." Miss Martineau tells me, "Some say it is inspired, some say it is mad." Exactly so; no *say* could be suitabler. But for you, my dear friend, I say and pray heartily: May God grant you strength; for you have a *fearful* work to do! Fearful I call it; and yet it is great, and the greatest. O for God's sake *keep yourself still quiet!* Do not hasten to write; you cannot be too slow about it. Give no ear to any man's praise or censure; know that that is *not* it: on the one side is as Heaven if you have strength to keep silent, and climb unseen; yet on the other side, yawning always at one's right-hand and one's left, is the frightfulest Abyss and Pandemonium! See Fenimore Cooper;—poor Cooper, he is *down in it*; and had a climbing faculty too. Be steady, be quiet, be in *no* haste; and God speed you well! My space is done.

Chelsea, 3 November, 1844.

The work itself [*Essays, Second Series*] falling on me by driblets has not the right chance yet—not till I get it in the bound state, and read it all at once—to produce its due impression on me. But I will say already of it, It is a *sermon* to me, as all your other deliberate utterances are; a real *word*, which I feel to be such,—alas, almost or altogether the one such, in a world all full of jargons, hearsays, echoes, and vain noises, which cannot pass with me for *words!* This is a praise far beyond any "literary" one; literary praises are not worth repeating in comparison.— For the rest, I have to object still (what you will call objecting against the Law of Nature) that we find you a Speaker indeed, but as it were a *Soliloquizer* on the eternal mountain-tops only, in vast solitudes where men and their affairs lie all hushed in a very dim remoteness; and only *the man* and the stars and the earth are visible,—whom, so fine a fellow seems he, we could perpetually punch into, and say, "Why won't you come and help us then? We have terrible need of one man like you down among us! It is cold and vacant up there; nothing paintable but rainbows and emotions; come down, and you shall do life-pictures, passions, facts,—which *transcend* all thought, and leave it stuttering and stammering!"—To which he answers that he won't, can't, and doesn't want to (as the Cockneys have it): and so I leave him, and say, "You Western Gymnosophist! Well, we can afford one man for that too. But—!"—By the bye, I ought to say, the sentences are very *brief*; and did not, in my *sheet* reading [of the printer's proofs], always entirely cohere for me. Pure genuine Saxon; strong and simple; of a clearness, of a beauty— But they did not, sometimes, rightly stick to their foregoers and their followers: the paragraph not as a beaten *ingot*, but as a beautiful square *bag of duck-shot* held together by canvas! I will try them again, with the Book deliberately before me. . . .

Chelsea, London, 2 March, 1847.

—I read your Book of Poems all faithfully, at Bay House (our Hampshire quarters); where the obstinate people,—with whom you are otherwise, in prose, a first favorite,—foolishly *refused* to let me read aloud; foolishly, for I would have made it mostly all plain by commentary:—so I had to read for myself; and can say, in spite of my hard-heartedness, I did gain, though under impediments, a real satisfaction and some tone of the Eternal Melodies sounding, afar off, ever and anon, in my ear! This is fact; a truth in Natural History; from which you are welcome to draw inferences. A grand View of the Universe, everywhere the sound (unhappily *far off,* as it were) of a valiant, genuine Human Soul: this, even under rhyme, is a satisfaction worth some struggling for. But indeed you are very perverse; and through this perplexed *un*-diaphanous element, you do not fall on me like radiant summer rainbows, like floods of sunlight, but with thin piercing radiances which affect me like the light of the *stars*. It is so: I wish you would become *concrete*, and write in prose the straightest way; but under any form I must put up with you; that is my lot. . . .

Chelsea, 2 December, 1856.

I got your book [*English Traits*] by post in the Highlands; and had such a day over it as falls rarely to my lot! Not for seven years and more have I got hold of such a Book;—Book by a real *man*, with eyes in his head; nobleness, wisdom, humor, and many other things, in the heart of him. Such Books do not turn up often in the decade, in the century. In fact I believe it to be worth all the Books ever written by New England upon Old. Franklin might have written such a thing (in his own way); no other since! We do very well with it here, and the wise part of us *best*. That Chapter on the Church is inimitable; "the Bishop asking a troublesome gentleman to take wine,"—you should see the kind of grin it awakens here on our best kind of faces. Excellent the manner of that, and the matter too dreadfully *true* in every part. I do not much seize your idea in regard to "Literature," though I do details of it, and will try again. Glad of that too, even in its half state; not "sorry" at *any* part of it,—you Sceptic! On the whole, write *again*, and ever again at greater length: there lies your only fault to me. And yet I know, that also is a right noble one, and rare in our day.

Chelsea, 29 January, 1861.

I read it [*The Conduct of Life*] a great while ago, mostly in sheets, and again read it in the finely printed form,—I can tell you, if you do not already guess, with a satisfaction given me by the Books of no other living mortal. I predicted to your English Bookseller a great sale even, reckoning it the best of all your Books. What the sale was or is I nowhere learned; but the basis of my prophecy remains like the rocks, and will remain. Indeed, except from my Brother John, I have heard no criticism that had much rationality,—some of them incredibly irrational (if that matter had not altogether become a barking of dogs among us);—but I always believe there are in the mute state a great number of thinking English souls, who can recognize a Thinker and a Sayer, of perennially human type, and welcome him as the rarest of miracles, in "such a spread of knowledge" as there now is:—one English soul of that kind there indubitably is; and I certify hereby, notarially if you like, that such is emphatically his view of the matter. You have grown older, more pungent, piercing;—I never read from you before such lightning-gleams of meaning as are to be found here. The finale of all, that of "Illusions" falling on us like snow-showers, but again of "the gods sitting steadfast on their thrones" all the while,—what a *Fiat Lux* is there, into the deeps of a philosophy, which the vulgar has not, which hardly three men living *have*, yet dreamt of! *Well done*, I say; and so let that matter rest.

From *The Correspondence of Thomas Carlyle and Ralph Waldo Emerson, 1834-1872* (Boston: Houghton Mifflin, 1883), I, 112-13, 141-43; II, 80-82, 151-52, 293-94, 311-12.

FRANCIS BOWEN

WE FIND beautiful writing and sound philosophy in this little work
[Emerson's *Nature*]; but the effect is injured by occasional vagueness of
expression, and by a vein of mysticism, that pervades the writer's whole
course of thought. The highest praise that can be accorded to it, is, that
it is a *suggestive* book, for no one can read it without tasking his
faculties to the utmost, and relapsing into fits of severe meditation. But
the effort of perusal is often painful, the thoughts excited are frequently bewildering, and the results to which they lead us, uncertain
and obscure. The reader feels as in a disturbed dream, in which shows
of surpassing beauty are around him, and he is conversant with disem-
bodied spirits, yet all the time he is harassed by an uneasy sort of
consciousness, that the whole combination of phenomena is fantastic
and unreal.

In point of taste in composition, some defects proceed from over
anxiety to avoid common errors. The writer aims at simplicity and
directness, as the ancient philosopher aimed at humility, and showed
his pride through the tatters of his cloak. He is in love with the Old
Saxon idiom, yet there is a spice of affectation in his mode of using it.
He is sometimes coarse and blunt, that he may avoid the imputation of
sickly refinement, and writes bathos with malice prepense, because he
abhors forced dignity and unnatural elevation.

These are grave charges, but we make them advisedly, for the author
knows better than to offend so openly against good taste, and, in many
passages of great force and beauty of expression, has shown that he can
do better. The following sentences, taken almost at random, will show
the nature of the defects alluded to.

"Now many are thought not only unexplained but inexplicable,
as language, sleep, dreams, beasts, sex."—p. 7.

"Standing on the bare ground, my head bathed by the blithe
air,—and uplifted into infinite space,—all egotism vanishes. I become a transparent eyeball."—p. 13. . . .

The purpose of the book, so far as it may be said to have a purpose,
is, to invite us to the observation of nature, and to point out manifesta-
tions of spirit in material existences and external events. The uses to

which the outward world is subservient are divided into four classes,
—Commodity, Beauty, Language, and Discipline. These ends the writer
considers as the final cause of every thing that exists, except the soul.
To the consideration of each he allots a chapter, and displays, often
with eloquence and a copious fund of illustration, the importance of
the end, and the aptitude of the means provided for its attainment. In
the latter part of the work, he seems disposed to neutralize the effect of
the former, by adopting the Berkeleyan system, and denying the outward and real existence of that Nature, which he had just declared to be
so subservient to man's spiritual wants. Of the chapters on "Spirit" and
"Prospects," with which the work concludes, we prefer not to attempt
giving an account, until we can understand their meaning.

From this sketch of the author's plan, it would seem, that he had
hardly aimed at originality. What novelty there is in the work, arises not
from the choice or distribution of the subject, but from the manner of
treatment. The author is not satisfied with that cautious philosophy
which traces the indirect influences of outward phenomena and physical laws on the individual mind, and contemplates the benevolence of
the Deity in particular instances of the adaptation and subserviency of
matter to spirit. He contemplates the Universe from a higher point of
view. Where others see only an analogy, he discerns a final cause. The
fall of waters, the germination of seeds, the alternate growth and decay
of organized forms, were not originally designed to answer the wants of
our physical constitution, but to acquaint us with the laws of mind, and
to serve our intellectual and moral advancement. The powers of Nature
have been forced into the service of man. The pressure of the atmosphere, the expansive force of steam, the gravity of falling bodies, are
our ministers, and do our bidding in levelling the earth, in changing a
wilderness into a habitable city, and in fashioning raw materials into
products available for the gratification of sense and the protection of
body. Yet these ends are only of secondary importance to the great
purpose for which these forces were created and made subject to
human power. Spiritual laws are typified in these natural facts, and are
made evident in the whole material constitution of things. Man must
study matter, that he may become acquainted with his own soul. . . .

In the chapter on "Discipline," the lessons of Nature are enforced
with great energy and directness. Man is not so constitutionally active,
but that he must receive repeated monitions to labor, or the powers of
body and mind will rust and decay. Wants and cravings are imposed
upon him, some of which his very physical constitution imperatively
requires to be satisfied, and immediate stinging pain is the punishment
of neglect. Once gratified, they recur, and provision must again be
made. To the knowledge of higher wants he arrives by more extended
observation and by every advance in knowledge. Thus, the thirst for
truth is insatiable, and increases from gratification. Nature entices us to

toil, by offering to gratify the lust for power, and subjecting herself to our dominion. She assumes the harness, and allows us to guide the reins, that she may carry us onward. An exact correspondence exists between the constitution of the soul and of the universe. The love of beauty, of dominion, of comfort, find their appropriate food in the various relations of things, that first called these passions into being, or at least first made us conscious of their existence. Variegated colors, brilliant appearances, curious forms, call us away from the chamber and the couch, that we may walk abroad and admire. The desire of fame and the social instinct are adapted to each other. Either principle alone would be inefficient and useless. United, they are continually pressing us to action. Industry is the great lesson of life, and the universe is the teacher.

But man is not only an active, but a moral being. The constitution of society, the relations which connect him with his fellows, are his instructers in virtue. A hermitage is no school of morals, and were man a hermit from his birth, the terms *right* and *wrong* with him would have but an imperfect and narrow application. The moral teachings of *Nature,* understanding by the term all that is distinct from spirit, are auxiliary, but insufficient. Mind must act upon mind. Man must stand in need of his fellow, before he can learn to love him. The mother, indeed, may love her child, before the infant is able to pay the first instalment of its debt to her, "risu cognoscere matrem." But the feeling is instinctive, and as such, is not a subject of moral approbation, any more than when it exists in the brute. With this limitation, we accept the following remarks from the book before us.

> "It has already been illustrated, in treating of the significance of material things, that every natural process is but a version of a moral sentence. The moral law lies at the centre of nature, and radiates to the circumference.... The moral influence of nature upon every individual is that amount of truth which it illustrates to him. Who can estimate this? Who can guess how much firmness the sea-beaten rock has taught the fisherman? how much tranquillity has been reflected to man from the azure sky, over whose unspotted deeps the winds for evermore drive flocks of stormy clouds, and leave no wrinkle or stain? how much industry and providence and affection we have caught from the pantomime of brutes? What a searching preacher of self-command is the varying phenomenon of health! "—pp. 53, 54.

Having thus considered the uses of the material world, its adaptation to man's physical wants, to his love of beauty, and his moral sense, the author turns and aims a back blow at the universe, which he has been leading us to admire and love. The heavens are rolled together like a scroll, the solid earth cracks beneath our feet,

Wide wilderness and mountain, rock and sea,
Peopled with busy transitory groups,"

are shadows, and exist only in mind. Matter is nothing, spirit is all. Man is alone in the vast inane with his God.

We have no quarrel with Idealism. Philosophers may form what dreams they choose, provided their speculations affect favorably their own faith and practice, and can never, from their very nature, command the belief, or bewilder the understanding of the mass of mankind. But we do protest against the implied assertion of the idealist, that the vulgar entertain opinions less philosophically just than his own. In the pride of opinion, he has overrated his own success, which at the utmost amounts only to this, that he has shown the inconclusiveness of the arguments commonly adduced to prove the outward and independent existence of matter. But he has brought no positive arguments to disprove the existence of any thing exterior to mind. He has not shown, that the common opinion involves any repugnancy or inconsistency in itself. The bridge on which we relied for support may be broken down, but we are not whelmed in the waters beneath. The belief still exists, and its universality is a fact for which the idealist cannot account. This fact puts the burden of proof upon him, and it is a load which he cannot support. The infant forms this belief before it quits its mother's arms. It has existed in every age, as a postulate for the exercise of many affections and emotions, that form a part of the primitive constitution of mind. Nay, the philosopher himself, "when he mingles with the crowd, must be content to comply with common opinions, to speak as custom dictates, and to forget, as well as he can, the doubts and the doctrines which reason perhaps permits, which speculation loves, and which solitude encourages."

On reviewing what we have already said of this singular work, the criticism appears to be couched in contradictory terms; we can only allege in excuse the fact, that the book is a contradiction in itself. . . . But enough of the work itself; it belongs to a class, and may be considered as the latest representative of that class.

Within a short period, a new school of philosophy has appeared, the adherents of which have dignified it with the title of Transcendentalism. In its essential features, it is a revival of the Old Platonic school. It rejects the aid of observation, and will not trust to experiment. The Baconian mode of discovery is regarded as obsolete; induction is a slow and tedious process, and the results are uncertain and imperfect. General truths are to be attained without the previous examination of particulars, and by the aid of a higher power than the understanding. "The hand-lamp of logic" is to be broken, for the truths which are *felt* are more satisfactory and certain than those which are *proved*. The sphere of intuition is enlarged, and made to comprehend not only mathematical axioms, but the most abstruse and elevated propositions respecting the being and destiny of man. Pure intelligence usurps the place of humble research. Hidden meanings, glimpses of spiritual and everlasting truth are found, where former observers sought only for natural facts. The observation of sensible phenomena can lead only to the discovery of insulated, partial, and relative laws; but the consideration of the same phenomena, in a typical point of view, may lead us to infinite and absolute truth,—to a knowledge of the reality of things.

As the object and method of philosophizing are thus altered, it is obvious that language also must be modified, and made to subserve other purposes than those for which it was originally designed. Transcendental philosophy took its rise in Germany, and the language of that country, from the unbounded power which it affords of composition and derivation from native roots, is well adapted to express results that are at once novel and vague. Hence the mysticism and over refinement, which characterize the German school of philosophy, art, and criticism. Our own tongue is more limited and inflexible. It must be enriched by copious importations from the German and Greek, before it can answer the ends of the modern school. And this has been done to such an extent, that could one of the worthies of old English literature rise from his grave, he would hardly be able to recognise his native tongue. . . .

We speak generally. To many writers of the New School we confess our obligation for new and valuable hints, expressed in energetic though affected language. But their influence is most pernicious. Writers, who cannot fathom their depth of thought, will imitate their darkness of language; and instead of comparing truths and testing propositions, readers must busy themselves in hunting after meaning, and investigating the significancy of terms.

It would avail but little, perhaps, with some Transcendentalists to assert, that the deepest minds have ever been the clearest, and to quote the example of Locke and Bacon, as of men who could treat the most abstruse subjects in the most familiar and intelligible terms.

From *The Christian Examiner and General Review* (Boston), 21 (Jan. 1837), 371-85.

SAMUEL OSGOOD

THE STRONG hold, which Coleridge and Wordsworth have taken, of so many minds, while it confers a high honor on their sublime genius, also shews, that they have but given expression to thoughts and feelings, which before existed and were growing in the minds of their readers. We rejoice at the influence of such poets. We rejoice that a poetry of Nature, truly Christian, is springing up among us. . . .

In our own bustling country, where banks, steam boats and rail roads seem to engross the nation's attention, we are happy to find some spirits, who keep aloof from the vulgar melee, and in calm of soul, live for Nature and for God. No greater exception to the common spirit of our nation, could be pointed out, than the author of a little work, recently published at the East. "Nature" is its title. . . .

The work is a remarkable one, and it certainly will be called remarkable by those, who consider it "mere moonshine," as well as those, who look upon it with reverence, as the effusion of a prophet-like mind. Whatever may be thought of the merits, or of the extravagances of the book, no one, we are sure, can read it, without feeling himself more wide awake to the beauty and meaning of Creation. . . .

The author is not such a dreamer on the beauties of the universe, as to forget its material uses. In the chapter on Commodity, he gives a view of the advantages, which our senses owe to Nature, as broad as if he were looking down on our earth with a mighty telescope, from some distant orb.

Is not the author right in considering Beauty one of the uses—one of the true final causes of Nature? Is not Beauty in itself merely considered one form of utility? Is there not a high utility, even in Beauty of outward form? Surely this simplest aspect of Beauty gives delight, and what gives inmost delight is truly useful. . . .

But a higher element than beauty of form, must be recognized, before we can see the full loveliness of Nature's beauty: [the spiritual unity of man and nature.]. . .

In the chapter on Language, Nature is considered the vehicle of thought. . . .

In this chapter on Language, the great law of correspondence, which runs through creation, is pointed out, that great law of analogy, which he, who shall understand truly, will know more of the universe, and be a wiser seer into the regions of undiscovered truth, than an eternity spent in groping round the world, endeavoring, without such light, to classify its scattered phenomena, could make him. . . .

In the last chapter on the uses of Nature—that on Discipline, the world around us is considered as disciplining our understanding and conscience. . . .

Coming to the chapter on Idealism, many will be tempted to shut the book in disgust, and lament, that so sensible a man as the writer has before shewn himself to be, should shew such folly. And we ourselves doubt much the wisdom of the speculation in this chapter, although we would not call him insane, who thinks the material world only ideal, believing as we do, that as Turgot has said, "He, who has never doubted the existence of matter, may be assured, he has no aptitude for metaphysical inquiries." We do not think, that Idealism leads to such dangerous conclusions, as are sometimes apprehended, since it implies no distrust in natural laws. The idealist, who believes matter to be only phenomenal, will conduct in exactly the same way, as the most thorough going materialist. The idealist will be just as cautious about cutting his finger, as the materialist will: for both will believe, that the pain is really felt, whatever they may think as to the finger or the knife being real or only apparent.

We are unable to perceive the bearing of the writer's argument, in proof of Idealism, or to allow the advantage, which he claims for his theory. All his arguments, it seems to us, go to prove merely the superiority of mind over matter. And all the advantage, which he claims for Idealism, is owned by that common spiritual philosophy, which subordinates matter to mind. We own there is much fine thought and good writing in this chapter, little as the sentiments agree with our Eclecticism. . . .

There are some things in this book, which we do ιot understand. The Orphic sentences at the end, "which a certain poet sang to the author," are especially dark to our misty vision. But probably the fault lies in ourselves. . . .

The many will call this book dreamy, and perhaps it is so. It may indeed naturally seem, that the author's mind is somewhat onesided, that he has not mingled enough with common humanity, to avoid running into eccentricity, that he has been so careful to keep his own individuality, that he has confounded his idiosyncrasies, with universal truth. All this may be. But it is not for the vulgar many to call such a man a dreamer. If he does dream, the many are more deluded dreamers. His dreams are visions of the eternal realities of the spiritual world: their's are of the fleeting phantoms of earth. Indeed the real visionary is not to be found, in the mystic's cell, or the philosopher's study, but in the haunts of busy life. The sensualist is a wretched visionary: he sees but a part, and that but a mean part of the reality of things, and sees all in a false light. The man of ambition is a dreamer. Those men, who pride themselves most on their practical turn of mind, are often far more visionary, than their more romantic neighbors, whom they are accustomed to deride. The veriest votary of Mammon, who makes himself an entire drudge to money getting, and boasts, that while other men are chasing shadows, such shadows, as beauty in nature and art, or truth in science or religion, he alone is grasping the substance; this man is constantly pursuing a phantom—he is chasing a joy, that never comes to him: . . . never finding the time, in which he may enjoy his wealth, he lives in a realm of illusion, until death, the stern teacher of reality, comes and touches him with his cold hand, and heaped treasures and fond visions at once disappear.

Not so with him, who puts his thoughts on things eternal. He sees the world as it really is. He looks on the temporal in the light of the Eternal. "So he comes to look on the world with new eyes." So he learns the high truths which nature teaches. Let us therefore hear the Orphic poet's saying:

" 'Build, therefore, your own world. As fast as you conform your life to the pure idea in your mind, that will unfold its great proportions. A correspondent revolution in things will attend the influx of the spirit.' "

From *The Western Messenger; Devoted to Religion and Literature* (Louisville), 2 (Jan. 1837), 385-93.

ORESTES AUGUSTUS BROWNSON

WE HAVE been not a little amused and somewhat edified by the various criticisms on this address ["The American Scholar"], which we have seen and heard of all kinds, from kindling admiration to gaping wonder, shrewd cavilling, sneering doubt, and even offended dignity. We wish, for ourselves, to express our hearty thanks to the author, to disburden our minds of a small load of censure, and utter some thoughts on the subject-matter of the address.

There are writers whom we should designate as in the twilight state, walking ever in an opposite direction to the motion of the earth—following with longing admiration the descending glory of the past—delighting in each tall peak, each floating cloud, which reflects the lustre of a fading day. To them the present is weary and worn, and the darkness and vapors steam up from the sunken vales of common life. There is a second class, in the midnight season of thought, lone and abstracted—watching the truths of eternity as they smile through far space on a darkened world. To them the present is the gleaming lights, the snatches of music, the distasteful clamor of foolish revelry, breaking harshly in upon their hour of rapt and solemn meditation. There is a third class, in morning wakefulness. Their gaze is on the brightening orient. They stand as *muezzins* on the mosques, as watchmen on the towers, summoning to prayer and work;—for the streaks of the dawning, and the golden flushes, are heralding the sun. The present is bright to them with hope; and the dewy incense promises fruitfulness, and the rising race are going forth to husband the garden of life. There is a fourth class, in the noonday and sunny cheerfulness, and clear light, of God's providence in the present time, on whose useful toil the *spirit of the age* shines down to ripen and to bless.

When we read a former production by the author of this address, we feared from its tone of somewhat exclusive and unsympathising contemplativeness, that he was of the second class. But we hail him now as one of the youthful expectants of a coming brighter hour of social life. Shall we not indeed say, that in his industry, and the unreserved communication of his best nature, as a preacher and lecturer, we gratefully recognise him as one of the working men of this generation? And yet would we see him more fully warmed with the great social idea of our era,—the great idea, which he has hinted at in this very address—of human brotherhood, of sonship to God....

We see, in Mr. Emerson, many traits befitting an American, that is, a Christian, free writer. He has deep faith in a heavenly Father of souls, reverence for each brother as a child of God,—respect for his own reason as a divine inspiration,—too much love for men to fear them,—a conscientious hungering and thirsting for truth,—and a serene trust in the triumph of good. He seems to us true, reverent, free, and loving. We cheerfully tolerate therefore any quaint trappings, in which a peculiar taste may lead him to deck his thoughts; and we pity the purists, who cannot see a manly spirit through a mantle not wholly courtly. At the same time we will freely express our regret that Mr. Emerson's style is so little a transparent one. There are no thoughts which may not be simply expressed. . . .The author of this address, we feel assured, does not willingly hide his thoughts from the poor vanity of being understood only by the initiated; and we have no doubt endeavors to be intelligible. He loves truth and respects man too well for such folly. . . .

Why then should he not open himself freely, simply? We think he means to do so. He cordially welcomes us to his high summits of speculation, and to the prospect they command, in full faith that our sight is keen as his. But he forgets that he has not pointed out the way by which he climbed. His conclusions are hinted, without the progressive reasonings through which he was led to them. Perhaps he does not come at them by any consecutive processes. They rather come to him unasked. To use his own language,

> "The new deed is yet a part of life,—remains for a time immersed in our unconscious life. In some contemplative hour, it detaches itself from the life, like a ripe fruit, to become a thought of the mind."—p. 13.

There are no developments of thought, there is no continuous flow in his writings. We gaze as through crevices on a stream of subterranean course, which sparkles here and there in the light, and then is lost. The style is in the extreme aphoristic. But again, another cause of his obscurity is a fondness for various illustration. He has a quick eye for analogies, and finds in all nature symbols of spiritual facts. His figures are occasionally so exquisitely felicitous, that we have hardly the heart to complain of this habit of mind, though, we confess, that not seldom we are attracted from the feature of his thoughts to the splendid jewelry of their attire, and yet oftener annoyed by the masquerade of rural or civic plainness, in which they see fit to march.

The subject of this Address is "The American Scholar," his training, duties, and prospects; and we cannot but wish that there had been more unity and order observed in treating it. The division is good—and the thoughts are apparently cast in a form. But the truth is, there is no progress, no onward stream. The best thoughts are not the leading but the incidental ones, and their arrangement might be varied without much altering the effect of the whole. But then these thoughts are fine ones, and there is a mass of them. And they might easily be run into shape, or rather built into a beautiful composition; or yet again grow naturally forth from the root of his central idea. This idea is variously expressed:

> "There is One Man—present to all particular men only partially; you must take the whole of society to find the whole man." "Man is one.". . . "The one thing of value in the world is the active soul,—the soul free, sovereign, active." "A nation of men, because each believes himself inspired by the Divine Soul which also inspires all men."

This fundamental truth, which Jesus felt, uttered, and lived as no disciple has ever faintly dreamed of, our author has apprehended with awe. It is a thought to open the fountains of the soul. . . .

> "We have listened too long to the courtly muses of Europe. The American freeman is already suspected to be timid, imitative, tame. Public and private avarice make the air we breathe thick and fat." "The scholar is decent, indolent, complaisant. There is no work for any but the decorous and the complaisant." "What is the remedy? If the single man will plant himself indomitably upon his instincts, and there abide, the huge world will come round to him. Patience— patience; with the shades of all the good and great for company; and for solace, the perspective of your own infinite life; and for work, the study and communication of principles, the making those instincts prevalent, the conversion of the world." "We will walk on our own feet, brothers and friends; we will work with our own hands; we will speak our own minds."

Now to our thinking this is high doctrine—timely, and well put. We trust all who have heard or read will lay it to heart, and go forth in the brightening day of a Christian, free literature with solemn purpose, patient resolve, cheerful hope, and forgiving tolerance; filled with the thought that, "God is working in them to will and do of his good pleasure;" and greeting each brother heir of immortality with a reverence and a benediction.

We have endeavored to give a skeleton of this, to us deeply interesting address, and now would proceed to remark upon the subject-matter itself. The theme proposed by the orator is the "AMERICAN SCHOLAR." Why did he not say AUTHOR? Every man is or should be a "student," "man thinking.". . . [Utilizing Emerson's terms and suggesting that Emerson might have emphasized the American as author rather than as scholar, Brownson urges at length the development of a great and democratic American literature.]

From *Boston Quarterly Review* (Boston), 1 (Jan. 1838), 106-20.

C. C. FELTON

THESE ESSAYS [*Essays, First Series*], we believe, are substantially the lectures which Mr. Emerson delivered last year in the city of Boston. They were listened to with delight by some, with distrust by others, and by a few with something like horror. Many young people imagined they contained the elements of a new and sublime philosophy, which was going to regenerate the world; many middle aged gentlemen and ladies shook their heads at the preaching of the new and dangerous doctrines, which they fancied they detected under Mr. Emerson's somewhat mystical and oracular phraseology; while the old and experienced saw nothing in the weekly rhapsody but blasphemy and atheism. It was not very easy to make out, from the varying reports of hearers, what these discourses really were; it was not much easier to say what they were, when you had heard them yourself; and the difficulty is not greatly diminished now they have taken the form of printed essays. One thing is very certain, that they excited no little attention among the philosophical quidnuncs of the good city of Boston, and drew around Mr. Emerson a circle of ardent admirers, not to say disciples, including many studious young men and accomplished young women; and that a great impulse has been given to speculations upon the weighty questions of man's nature and destiny. Among the observable effects of this new impulse, is a general extravagance of opinion, which accompanies all strong intellectual excitements, and an overweening self-confidence on the part of many inexperienced people of both sexes, who have taken upon themselves to doubt and dispute everything, that the experience of the human race has seemed to establish. To a very great extent, the new opinions, if such they may be called, are ancient errors and sophistries, mistaken for new truths, and disguised in the drapery of a misty rhetoric, which sorely puzzles the eye of the judgment. . . . Unquestionably, some of the best writing of late years has proceeded from the pens of authors, whom the public call, for want of a better name, Transcendentalists. Mr. Emerson is not to be confounded with any class, though he has strong affinities with the transcendentalists. He is an extravagant, erratic genius, setting all authority at defiance, sometimes writing with the pen of an angel, (if angels ever write,) and sometimes gravely propounding the most amazing nonsense. To subject his writings to any of the common critical tests, would be absurd. He would probably laugh in the critic's face.

The Essays cannot be said to contain any system of religion, morals, or philosophy. The most that can be affirmed is, that they are full of significant hints upon all these subjects, from which the author's opinions, so far as he has any, may be inferred. But he has expressed such sovereign contempt for consistency, that we must not look for that virtue in what he may choose to say; if we do, we shall look in vain. In its place, we shall very often encounter point-blank contradictions; a thing very strongly said in one essay, and very strongly unsaid in the next. We find no fault with this, as the essayist has given us fair warning. But we would remark, that a writer, whose opinions are so variable, cannot wonder if they have but little value in the eyes of the world. We are perpetually struck, also, with a boldness, bordering close upon rashness, in dealing with matters which men do not usually approach, without a sense of awe. We doubt not, the feelings of many readers have been shocked by an appearance of irreverence, with which the most momentous themes are sometimes handled in this volume; an error of taste, at least, quite unnecessary to any of the aims of the freest discussion. The name of Jesus is repeatedly coupled with that of Socrates, and other great philosophers and thinkers, as if he had been on a level with them, and no more; a mere teacher, philanthropist, or system-maker. Possibly such may be Mr. Emerson's opinion; but it almost seems as if he studied this collocation of names for the purpose of startling the common sentiment of reverence for the sacred person of the founder of our religion. With many of Mr. Emerson's leading views we differ entirely, if we understand them; if we do not, the fault lies in the author's obscurity. His general doctrine, for example, with regard to the instincts, and the influence which they ought to have upon our daily conduct, is one, which, if acted upon, would overturn society, and resolve the world into chaos. The view of human nature, on which such a doctrine alone can rest, is countenanced neither by reason nor revelation, neither by individual nor national experience. . . .

Mr. Emerson writes in a very uncommon style. His associations are curious and subtle, and his words are often chosen with singular felicity. Some of his sentences breathe the most exquisite music, of which language is capable. His illustrations are in most cases highly poetical. An intense love of nature, and a keen perception of the beauties of the external world, are manifested on every page of his writings. But the effect of his powers of style is not a little diminished by a studied quaintness of language, acquired apparently by imitating the turns of expression in the old English authors, more frequently than becomes a man of original genius. . . . He is often quaint where there is no peculiar solemnity or gravity or originality of thought, to which the quaintness is a suitable accompaniment. He sometimes picks up a phrase that has not been used since Shakspeare, and is quite unintelligible without a glossary. His writings are thickly studded with oddities, gathered from the most unfrequented by-paths of English literature; and when we add to this the super-sublimated transcendentalism of the Neo-Platonistic style, which he now and then affects, we must not wonder if Mr. Emerson's phraseology frequently passes the comprehension of the vulgar. Moreover, he plays certain tricks with words, which disfigure his pages not a little. . . . To illustrate our meaning, we will give but one example. It is a trick very easily performed by any second-rate juggler, being nothing more than a collocation of words slightly differing from the natural one. "Always the thought is prior to the fact;" "always the soul hears an admonition;" and so on, fifty times or more. This is caught up by the smaller writers. Always Mr. Emerson writes so, and always the admiring chorus do the same. . . .

There is great refinement of feeling often shown in Mr. Emerson's essays, and occasionally a noble appreciation of the dignity of the human soul, and of the high relations of man to man. But even his views upon these he carries to an impracticable length. He underrates the value of all positive institutions, and indulges in a very unbecoming and undeserved tone of sarcasm against them. . . . The institutions, which philanthropic men have built up to relieve the woes of suffering humanity, to spread the blessings of knowledge among the ignorant, and to raise the fallen from their low estate, are among the brightest proofs, that the spirit of Christianity is better understood now than it has been at any former time; and, though they may be made now and then the theatre for pompous fools to display their ostentatious charities upon; yet they are, on the whole, noble expressions of the universal brotherhood of man, and far too good to be set aside for the claims of individual dignity and an imaginary independence, so extravagantly urged by Mr. Emerson.

Mr. Emerson's whimsical associations often lead him out of the regions of thought, into the realm of vague, shadowy impressions. We read paragraph after paragraph, and upon closing the book can no more recall our author's meaning, than the cloudy images of a dream. We may be told, the fault is ours; and Dr. Johnson's famous piece of boorishness may be significantly hinted at, as it has been a great many times; "Sir, I am bound to furnish you with reasons, but not with brains." We do not admit the force of the reply. The greatest writers, of all languages, are the most distinguished for their simplicity and intelligibleness; but third and fourth-rate men love to separate themselves from the mass, and to shroud their meaning, if they have any, in a sacred and awful mysticism. . . . Shakspeare is perfectly easy to understand, except where his text is corrupted, or where he alludes to some forgotten opinion or custom of his age; but Coleridge is fond of piling up big-sounding words, which pass with many people for sublimity; truly a very different sublimity from that of Homer and Shakspeare. Something like this we confess we find at times in Mr. Emerson's writings. It may arise from an effort to express what no human speech can express. Undoubtedly, there are refinements of thought and feeling, which the individual soul, in certain transient moods, apprehends, but which words fail utterly to convey to others. Such refinements make up the reveries of a summer evening; such are the moods of the mind in that agreeable semi-somnambulic state, between sleeping and waking, rather nearer the former, however, than the latter. But it requires a mighty effort of the waking man to attach any definite thought to them, when the dreamy crisis is past. And so it requires an equal effort for a person of plain understanding to make out clearly the sense of many of Mr. Emerson's musical paragraphs. . . .

Nothing can be more unsound than the philosophy of the Essay on Spiritual Laws. If it is true, we must believe, that man should be left to grow up like the oak or the wild-horse, instead of being carefully trained, and taught that he is a moral agent, endowed with the mighty powers of will, and bound to obey the voice of conscience. But there are many amusing things ingeniously said in this essay; amusing from their very extravagance. . . .

The Essay under the affected title of the Over-Soul is the most objectionable of all of them, both with regard to sentiment and style. Not that it can do any great harm; such speculations are too vague, too unreal for that.

We think Mr. Emerson's readers will be entertained, if not instructed, by his volume. Some, no doubt, will imagine, that it is going to turn the world upside down. We have no such apprehensions. It has not the force and fervor, the passionate appeals and popular tact, to work thus upon men's minds; but it contains many single thoughts of dazzling brilliancy; much exquisite writing, and a copious vein of poetical illustration; and shows many indications of manly character and independent thinking; but from the praises, which the author's genius would otherwise deserve, large deductions must be made, on the score of oddity, whim, and affectation; and particularly on the score of great levity of opinion, and rashness of speculation on the gravest subjects.

From *The Christian Examiner and General Review* (Boston), 30 (May 1841), 253-62.

C. A. BARTOL

WE COME now to by far the most original and peculiar of these volumes [under review], the poems by Mr. Emerson. To his genius, considered in its peculiarity, we bow. We own the spell which, more powerfully perhaps than any other American writer, he has thrown over our fancy. We know of nothing in the whole range of modern writers superior in original merit to his productions. He is "of imagination all compact." To read his finer pieces is to our poetic feeling like receiving a succession of electric shocks; and each additional line in them, communicating subtilely with all the rest, multiplies the force of this ideal battery. He is so frugal of language, as to let no phrase stand which is not charged with meaning. His merit, however, is not uniform. He is sometimes trivial in his themes, but never weak or wordy in their treatment. He is occasionally vague and mystical, but the brilliant distinctness usual in his thoughts and illustrations we take for proof that all his sentences refer to something real in his own mind. His best strokes cut below the superficial impressions made upon us by ordinary writers, and chisel themselves in the memory; while the softest musical rhythm is often so connected with the sharply arranged parsimony of his words, that passages repeat themselves in our involuntary recollection, as in the mysteriously sounding chambers of the spirit we hear over and over again the tunes of some great master. We are always glad to confess our obligation for intellectual helps, and we have to thank Mr. Emerson for the strong flashes of wit and sense, clad in bright imagery, with which he has often waked our minds from slumber. His discernment is as keen as his invention is fruitful. No man has a finer eye than he to trace those secret lines of correspondence which run through and bind together all parts of this lower frame of things. And even when we have been in the very spot in the realms of thought where he pitches his tent, he will detect some hidden analogy, and surprise us with a new observation. We know of no compositions that surpass his in their characteristic excellence. Even his unshaped fragments are not bits of glass, but of diamond, and have always the true poetic lustre, an inward gleam like that playing amid the layers of a sea-shell. Some of his conceptions are turned into as admirable expression as we find in Milton's sonnets or Shakespeare's songs.

We have thus praised this writer, and, as some may think, overpraised him, in the sincerity of our hearts. Our reference has, we find, unconsciously included his prose as well as his poetry. But they are both of a piece, and bear alike the stamp of their author's intellectual unity. The same affluent and over-mastering imagination, the same grasp of all the powers of language, the same faithful report from sight and experience, prevail throughout all his productions. But our criticism must find fault with the same frankness with which it bestows eulogy, and will be for that but the more prized by our friend's magnanimous spirit. He has, we think, more height than breadth. He shoots up like the pinnacle of an *aiguille* mountain into the atmosphere of the great poets, but he lacks altogether their various richness and comprehensive proportions. He is dry and cold in the comparison. The productive fields do not so spread out below the frosty cone of inaccessible sublimity which towers above. . . . The heart in his poetry is less than the head, and this causes a deficiency for which nothing else can fully atone. Only a transcendent splendor and wealth of intellect could redeem many of his pieces from condemnation and forgetfulness, as being frigid and unfeeling. These are sad flaws in such noble workmanship. Did a fellow-feeling for human nature in all its varieties equal and fill out his other traits, we might think the great poet of America had been born, to bring on our flourishing Augustan age. . . .

And yet we hardly know how he could have the kind of human sympathy which we most value for the inspiration of such an undertaking, with his present views of religion. There is no recognition in his pages of the Christian faith, according to any, however catholic, idea of it which we are able to form. He seems to have no preference of Jesus over any other great and good man. . . . He does not even appear to own any distinction between man and Deity. He talks of "the gods" as an old Roman would do. One personal Creator is not present to his thought. He does not go for the signs of such a Being into the broad circumference of his works, but confines himself within the little rim of his own individual consciousness. He puts aside Bible and ritual, and all human speech and outward light, for the "supersolar beam." In religion he fills the whole space of thought with that mystic element, which we must perhaps admit, but should confine in a corner. He does not, with a plain trust, examine the world which God has made, but curiously inspects the inverted image of it upon his own mental retina. He does not pay to the instincts of mankind or of society the respect he would render to the peculiar instincts of the animal, the bee or the beaver. And not taking cordially to his heart the Christian doctrines of a Father and a particular Providence, how can he strongly embrace the dependent doctrine of human brotherhood, or feel the unlimited sympathy which this doctrine inspires? We speak here, of course, of his system. We doubt not the kindness of his actual relations with men. We believe a hearty historical faith in Christianity would add greatly to the power of his genius. . . .

We ought, however, to say, that the noblest principles of conduct are often asserted in his pages. We rejoice to find instances of a truly grand morality, and surpassing expressions of a pure and beautiful spirit; but are suddenly perplexed, as we proceed, by an optimism confounding all moral distinctions. He seems, in some places, to know no difference between light and darkness, sweet and bitter. . . .

There is an undertone of sadness running through these rhymes, sometimes harsh and scornful, and sometimes tender and refined, like angelic melancholy. We fancy this, too, may proceed from the peculiarity of the writer's belief. Seldom do we hear from him the truly cheerful strain which an earnest faith in Christianity would prompt. In that marvellously beautiful "Threnody," near the close of the book, the sorrow at the commencement is out of all proportion to the comfort at the end. It is the song of a stricken and struggling stoicism. . . . We remember in all our reading nothing more cheerless. . . . Let him in lowliness receive these [comforts of God], and then, for the "Threnody," and the "Dirge" which precedes it, we should hope to receive lines as highly adorned with the lights of a creative fancy, but gilded from above also by the beams of heaven. There would at least be nothing in them of the "grief whose balsam never grew."

But we must pause. The analysis of Mr. Emerson's writings is no short or easy task. We would not pretend to oversee his summit, but only to note our impressions as we stand and contemplate it. His works, on account of their peculiarity, if nothing else, will probably be among the most enduring of the present time. There is much in them to admire and be improved by. And while we must think there is much also that is unsound and must be injurious to any mind imbibing it, we intend no personal commendation in expressing our conviction that he is a true-minded and righteous man, raised above every thing unworthy and living a blameless life according to the monitions of his own conscience. Our calling is not to speak of the man, but of the author. We think the intellectual states and tendencies which we have noted chill and cripple his genius. . . . Would he fetch an echo from the universal heart, as it beats in the breasts of men from generation to generation, he must add to his style a faith and fervor as signal as its brilliancy and force.

We must retire from our survey of these fruits of Mr. Emerson's labors. And as we retire, the traits we have objected to fade away from our attention, and many a melodious note from "Each in All," "The Problem," "The Humble-Bee," "Monadnoc," and "The Forerunners," lingers and renews itself pleasantly in our ear.

But having been constrained in our criticism of Mr. Emerson's volume to suggest radical objections as well as to confess strong admiration, we feel it to be right that we should here try to characterize very briefly his mind. Poetry with him is no recreation or trial of skill, but the sincerity and very substance of his soul; it shows not the passing figures of a magic-lantern, but the convictions and views of life for which he would be a martyr. What, then, is the mind that we see on his page? It is a mind subtile, brilliant, rapid, and decisive. It is a mind in which intuition takes the place of logic, and an insatiable aspiration banishes every form of philosophy. The lightning of his genius reveals the landscape of his thought, and the darkness quickly swallows it up again, till another flash reveals more or less of it. It is a mind scorning forms, conventions, and institutions, and, if it could have its way, would substitute for all this stable platform of law and custom on which we live and work the extemporaneous impulses of the spirit. It is a mind that despises all that has been done, and regards the highest and most inspired utterances of men as but "syllables" dropping carelessly from the tongue; and holds in slight esteem achievements to which even itself is not equal, except in the dreamily anticipated efforts of some distant time and unknown world to come. It sees an ideal which makes it contemn all that is actual. It draws upon the well of its own conceptions, and deems that single draught will suffice though it pass by all other fountains. It aims at a lonely, insulated being, shut up to what may come to it from the general life of the universe, and prizes all foreign helps from its fellows only in proportion to their accordance with its independent results. It weighs and oversees, in its own notion, all characters of intellect and virtue that ever were, and Jesus Christ as confidently as the rest. As we might expect, the consequence of these tendencies is much narrowness, a very partial and unfair estimate of other and differing minds, great injustice in many respects to existing arrangements and instrumentalities, and a continual rising above the useful agencies of life into an atmosphere too rarefied to support any organization less singular than his. But let us more gladly observe, in addition to these things, moral courage, fearless candor, freedom from vanity and from many false leanings, if he has not reached all that are true.

From *The Christian Examiner and Religious Miscellany* (Boston), 42 (March 1847), 255-61.

C. E. NORTON

THE PRESENT volume [*Representative Men*] is marked strongly both
by the excellences and defects of Mr. Emerson's other writings. His
style is often musical, clear, and brilliant; words are selected with so
rare a felicity that they have the shine of diamonds, and they cut their
meaning on the reader's mind as the diamond's edge leaves its trace
deep and sharp on the surface of glass. But by and by, we fall upon a
passage which either conveys no distinct sense, or in which some very
common-place thought is made to sound with the clangor of a braying
trumpet. Quaintness of thought and expression is his easily besetting
sin; and here lies the secret of his sympathy with Carlyle, that highly
gifted master of oddity and affectation. As a writer, Mr. Emerson is
every way Carlyle's superior, would he but let the Carlylese dialect
alone. He has more imagination, more refinement and subtlety of
thought, more taste in style, more exquisite sense of rhythm. Perhaps
his range of intellectual vision is not so broad. He has not the learning
of Carlyle, nor the abundant humor, which sometimes reconciles us
even to absurdity. But Mr. Emerson has a more delicate wit, a wit often
quite irresistible by its unexpected turns, and the sudden introduction
of effective contrasts. Carlyle has an extraordinary abundance of words,
a store of epithets, good, bad, and indifferent, by which the reader is
often flooded; Emerson is more temperate and artistic. And yet we
catch him, every now and then, mimicking the Scotchman, as if Carlyle
were the master, and Emerson the pupil. He imitates Carlyle's affectation of odd and quaint expressions; he imitates him in the structure of
his sentences; he imitates him in borrowing from the Germans a transcendental coloring, and in putting on an air of indifference to all
positive opinions, an assumption of even-handed impartiality towards
all religious systems. The trick of grotesque illustration by common or
vulgar objects, he has caught from the Platonic Socrates. But setting
aside these imitations and affectations, there hovers over much of his
writing a peculiar and original charm, drawn from no source but the
delicate and beautiful mind of the author himself.

The six men, who are here brought forward as representative characters, are Plato, Swedenborg, Montaigne, Shakspeare, Napoleon, and
Goethe. At first sight, the choice appears a little whimsical, as to some,
at least, of the members of this representative body. The number is

certainly small, and the names are select enough—an oligarchy which we
suspect the republic of letters would be slow to submit to. We see, with
regard to two or three of them, the personal sympathies of the author,
as in Montaigne and Swedenborg. In the delineation of the characters of
these six representatives, we find much knowledge, frequent brilliancy
of expression, followed by intense darkness, and flashes of thought that
shoot up like streams of fire from volcanoes in the night. But on the
whole, they are rather attempts to set forth qualities of character than
to represent characters. The effect is, in every case, fragmentary. They
are like the studies of an artist, who has painted portions of his picture
on separate bits of canvas, and then, instead of combining them into a
great and harmonious whole by working them together under the inspiration of a general idea, stitches the sundered members as chance
may arrange them. We do not, therefore, rise from the study of any one
of them with an idea of it as an organic whole. There is no method, no
unity of effect, though there are separate and inimitable felicities of
execution. . . .

There is also a tone of exaggeration in the exhibition of each man's
peculiar qualities. The true position of these individual representatives
in the intellectual history of the world is not correctly given; at least, so
it seems to us. For instance, though one can hardly overstate the *genius*
of Plato, understanding by that word the sum total of his natural and
acquired gifts, yet the first sentence of the lecture on Plato is a mon-
strous piece of overdone assertion. "Among books," says Emerson,
"Plato only is entitled to Omar's fanatical compliment to the Koran,
when he said, 'Burn the libraries, for their value is in this book.' " And
again, "Out of Plato come all things that are still written and debated
among men of thought."

Part of this vivid rhetoric is perhaps due to the exigencies of the
lecture form. One is always tempted, while addressing a popular
audience, to heighten the truth for the sake of deepening the effect.
But making all proper deductions from the statements on this ground,
is the residue correct and sound? To say nothing of great modern
thinkers, who have mastered regions of thought which Plato never
dreamed of,—did Plato include his immediate successor, Aristotle?
Surely not. . . .

In the course of this lecture, we are entertained with a portrait of
Socrates. This also is an exaggeration; that is, the whole effect is wide
of the true impression which that great martyr-philosopher ought to
leave upon the mind. Socrates had the whimsical peculiarities which Mr.
Emerson delineates; but they were far from being such prominent and
essential parts of him, as they appear in this sketch. Plato used the
name of Socrates, and the witty, arguing, questioning characteristics of
his daily life, because precisely these were the most dramatic—precisely
these answered the end of Plato's art. But a justly proportioned figure

of Socrates can only be made by combining the three representations of Plato, Xenophon, and Aristophanes;—the first for the peculiarities of his talk, for his lofty and inflexible morality, for his religious earnestness; the second for a historical account of the man; and the third for a parody upon his personal peculiarities and his modes of dealing with the minds of others. . . . With these preliminary "monitions to the reader," we commend the passage to which we refer, as a pleasant piece of whimsical exaggeration. . . .

We have merely touched upon a striking peculiarity of Mr. Emerson, in a religious point of view—his apparent indifference to positive religious belief, as shown by his manner of classing all beliefs together. When Christ and Socrates are spoken of in the same breath, we wonder that the military exploits, the exclusive love of Athens, the neglect of domestic duties, the humor, the drollery, and the drinking bouts of the latter do not rise in strange contrast with the universality that embraced Jew and Gentile alike in the arms of divine love, the sad and gentle earnestness to which a jest would be a profanation, and the awful authority that went with our Lord as from on high, compelling the hearers of his word to cry out that "never man spake like this man." And more still do we wonder, when Mahomet and the Saviour are classed together as religious geniuses and reformers, that those who so contemplate them do not feel the shocking incongruity of placing the serene, self-denying, and spotless life of the one—even if we regard him as but a man—his pure and peaceful teachings, which stopped not at outward acts, but pierced to the root of wickedness in the heart, side by side with the worldly ambition, the violence, the imposture, the shedding of blood, the fierce and exclusive bigotry, and the insatiable licentiousness of the other.

From *The North American Review* (Boston), 70 (April 1850), 520-24.

ANONYMOUS

MR. EMERSON'S book [*English Traits*], did it profess to describe all of England, would be justly open to the severest criticism. It ignores pauperism, ignorance, and crime, aristocratic pretension and plebeian sycophancy, sinecure laziness and under-paid labor,—in fine, all the inequalities of condition, realized right, and availing privilege, which assimilate the moral and social landscape of Great Britain much more nearly to the broken surface of Switzerland, than to the gentle alternations of hill and valley on its own soil. But all of the less pleasing "English traits" have been set forth with ample minuteness of detail by the greater portion of recent travellers, and we are glad to open one book that revives our early pride in our mother-land, and makes us feel anew the unparalleled queenliness of her position and belongings. . . .

With the intense *subjectivism* of Mr. Emerson's philosophy we are at swords' points. We hesitate not to say, that, pushed to its legitimate consequences, it neutralizes moral distinctions, eliminates duty and accountability, obliterates religion, and excludes the conception of a personal and self-conscious Deity. And even in the book before us, when religious or ethical subjects are touched upon, (which they are but seldom, and lightly,) we discern traces of the indifferentism which proceeds from the author's philosophy. But this very element is propitious to merely aesthetic observation and impression. Mr. Emerson threw open his own broad, rich, delicately organized, and generously cultured intellect, with an Argus-eyed passiveness, with a receptivity which no emotion or affection weakened or distorted, to take the exact impress of what he heard and saw.

The greatness of England is in fact the theme of all his chapters. And there are many aspects in which she is the greatest of the nations. She has enriched herself with the spoils of every zone and soil. Her language, a conglomerate from all the tongues of ancient and modern civilization, is the type of her national personality and genius. With hardly a tithe of the learning of Germany, she is the fountain of elegant scholarship. With often a paucity and never a redundance of creative talent, her literature embodies the wealth and beauty of all times and lands. Inferior to France in science, she immeasurably transcends her in its concrete forms and practical uses. Later than the Continental nations in almost every branch of lucrative industry, she has domesticated all their processes, and has made her manufactures the staple of the world's commerce. Limited in her natural resources, she supplements them by the empire of the sea, and the lordship of the tropics and the Orient. What her arms might fail of, her diplomacy secures. . . . Every decaying timber in her political and social fabric is so buttressed, that it cannot fall till slow time disintegrates it; every weak member of the pile is so built around and over, that it bears no strain.

Mr. Emerson gives few details of his English sojourn. The titles of his chapters are such general heads of remark as "Land," "Race," "Manners," "Wealth," "Aristocracy," "Religion." Under each he gives rather the sum total of his observations, than the specific instances that served for his generalizations. He delights in antithesis and contrast, and brings out with unequalled rhetorical force very many of the anomalies of the English commonwealth and society,—those balancings and co-workings of seemingly opposite and antagonistic forces, by which strength is born out of weakness, and the ever fresh and new from decadence and decline. . . .

Mr. Emerson has been twice in England. His second voyage thither was in 1847, at the invitation of several Mechanics' Institutes in Lancashire and Yorkshire, to deliver a series of lectures. The greater part of the work purports to give the impressions received during the tour made in pursuance of and in connection with that engagement. His first chapter, however, is devoted to an earlier visit, in 1833, and is chiefly filled with his interviews with persons well known in the literary world, such as Landor, Coleridge, Carlyle, and Wordsworth. He does not heighten our reverence for Coleridge, who overwhelmed him with a torrent of windy declamation, fraught with the intensest egotism and the stalest commonplaces. "The visit," says Mr. Emerson, "was rather a spectacle than a conversation, of no use beyond the satisfaction of my curiosity. He was old and preoccupied, and could not bend to a new companion and think with him." His visit to Wordsworth afforded him much greater edification, and presents the same amiable picture, so often given us, of the simple, true, kind, reverent old man, full of unconscious oddities, and, with virgin modesty, not one whit less egotistical than the pompous philosopher of Highgate.

From *The North American Review* (Boston), 83 (Oct. 1856), 505-10.

JAMES RUSSELL LOWELL

IT IS a singular fact, that Mr. Emerson is the most steadily attractive lecturer in America. . . . A lecturer now for something like a third of a century, one of the pioneers of the lecturing system, the charm of his voice, his manner, and his matter has never lost its power over his earlier hearers, and continually winds new ones in its enchanting meshes. What they do not fully understand they take on trust, and listen . . .

We call it a singular fact, because we Yankees are thought to be fond of the spread-eagle style, and nothing can be more remote from that than his. We are reckoned a practical folk, who would rather hear about a new air-tight stove than about Plato; yet our favorite teacher's practicality is not in the least of the Poor Richard variety. . . . if he were to make an almanac, his directions to farmers would be something like this: "OCTOBER: *Indian Summer*; now is the time to get in your early Vedas." What, then, is his secret? Is it not that he out-Yankees us all? that his range includes us all? that he is equally at home with the potato-disease and original sin, with pegging shoes and the Over-soul? that, as we try all trades, so has he tried all cultures? and above all, that his mysticism gives us a counterpoise to our super-practicality?

There is no man living to whom, as a writer, so many of us feel and thankfully acknowledge so great an indebtedness for ennobling impulses,—none whom so many cannot abide. What does he mean? ask these last. Where is his system? What is the use of it all?. . . I will only say that one may find grandeur and consolation in a starlit night without caring to ask what it means, save grandeur and consolation; one may like Montaigne, as some ten generations before us have done, without thinking him so systematic as some more eminently tedious (or shall we say tediously eminent?) authors; one may think roses as good in their way as cabbages . . .

The bother with Mr. Emerson is, that, though he writes in prose, he is essentially a poet. . . . We look upon him as one of the few men of genius whom our age has produced, and there needs no better proof of it than his masculine faculty of fecundating other minds. Search for his eloquence in his books and you will perchance miss it, but meanwhile you will find that it has kindled all your thoughts. For choice and pith of language he belongs to a better age than ours, and might rub shoulders with Fuller and Browne . . . His eye for a fine, telling phrase that will carry true is like that of a backwoodsman for a rifle; and he will dredge you up a choice word from the mud of Cotton Mather himself. A diction at once so rich and so homely as his I know not where to match in these days of writing by the page. . . . As in all original men, there is something for every palate. . . .

The announcement that such a pleasure as a new course of lectures by him is coming, to people as old as I am, is something like those forebodings of spring that prepare us every year for a familiar novelty, none the less novel, when it arrives, because it is familiar. We know perfectly well what we are to expect from Mr. Emerson, and yet what he says always penetrates and stirs us, as is apt to be the case with genius, in a very unlooked-for fashion. Perhaps genius is one of the few things which we gladly allow to repeat itself,—one of the few that multiply rather than weaken the force of their impression by iteration? . . . At sixty-five . . . he has that privilege of soul which abolishes the calendar, and presents him to us always the unwasted contemporary of his own prime. I do not know if he seem old to his younger hearers, but we who have known him so long wonder at the tenacity with which he maintains himself even in the outposts of youth. I suppose it is not the Emerson of 1868 to whom we listen. For us the whole life of the man is distilled in the clear drop of every sentence, and behind each word we divine the force of a noble character, the weight of a large capital of thinking and being. We do not go to hear what Emerson says so much as to hear Emerson. Not that we perceive any falling-off in anything that ever was essential to the charm of Mr. Emerson's peculiar style of thought or phrase. The first lecture, to be sure, was more disjointed even than common. It was as if, after vainly trying to get his paragraphs into sequence and order, he had at last tried the desperate expedient of *shuffling* them. It was chaos come again, but it was a chaos full of shooting-stars, a jumble of creative forces. The second lecture, on "Criticism and Poetry," was quite up to the level of old times, full of that power of strangely-subtle association whose indirect approaches startle the mind into almost painful attention, of those flashes of mutual understanding between speaker and hearer that are gone ere one can say it lightens. The vice of Emerson's criticism seems to be, that while no man is so sensitive to what is poetical, few men are less sensible than he of what makes a poem. He values the solid meaning of thought above the subtler meaning of style. He would prefer Donne, I suspect, to Spenser, and sometimes mistakes the queer for the original.

To be young is surely the best, if the most precarious, gift of life; yet there are some of us who would hardly consent to be young again, if it were at the cost of our recollection of Mr. Emerson's first lectures during the consulate of Van Buren. We used to walk in from the country to the Masonic Temple (I think it was), through the crisp winter night, and listen to that thrilling voice of his, so charged with subtle meaning and subtle music, as shipwrecked men on a raft to the hail of a ship that came with unhoped-for food and rescue. Cynics might say what they liked. Did our own imaginations transfigure dry remainder-biscuit into ambrosia? At any rate, he brought us *life*, which, on the whole, is no bad thing. Was it all transcendentalism? magic-lantern pictures on mist? As you will. Those, then, were just what we wanted. But it was not so. The delight and the benefit were that he put us in communication with a larger style of thought, sharpened our wits with a more pungent phrase, gave us ravishing glimpses of an ideal under the dry husk of our New England; made us conscious of the supreme and everlasting originality of whatever bit of soul might be in any of us; freed us, in short, from the stocks of prose in which we had sat so long that we had grown wellnigh contented in our cramps. And who that saw the audience will ever forget it, where every one still capable of fire, or longing to renew in them the half-forgotten sense of it, was gathered? Those faces, young and old, agleam with pale intellectual light, eager with pleased attention, flash upon me once more . . . I hear again that rustle of sensation, as they turned to exchange glances over some pithier thought, some keener flash of that humor which always played about the horizon of his mind like heat-lightning . . .

To some of us that long-past experience remains as the most marvellous and fruitful we have ever had. Emerson awakened us, saved us from the body of this death. It is the sound of the trumpet that the young soul longs for, careless what breath may fill it. . . . Nor did it blow retreat, but called to us with assurance of victory. Did they say he was disconnected? So were the stars, that seemed larger to our eyes, still keen with that excitement, as we walked homeward with prouder stride over the creaking snow. And were *they* not knit together by a higher logic than our mere sense could master? Were we enthusiasts? I hope and believe we were, and am thankful to the man who made us worth something for once in our lives. If asked what was left? what we carried home? we should not have been careful for an answer. It would have been enough if we had said that something beautiful had passed that way. . . .

Few men have been so much to so many, and through so large a range of aptitudes and temperaments, and this simply because all of us value manhood beyond any or all other qualities of character. We may suspect in him, here and there, a certain thinness and vagueness of quality, but let the waters go over him as they list, this masculine fibre of his will keep its lively color and its toughness of texture. I have heard some great speakers and some accomplished orators, but never any that so moved and persuaded men as he. There is a kind of undertow in that rich baritone of his that sweeps our minds from their foothold into deeper waters with a drift we cannot and would not resist.

From "Emerson the Lecturer" in *My Study Windows* (Boston: James R. Osgood, 1871), pp. 375-84.

Nineteenth-Century Perspectives

THEODORE PARKER

MR. EMERSON is the most American of our writers. The Idea of America, which lies at the bottom of our original institutions, appears in him with great prominence. We mean the idea of personal freedom, of the dignity and value of human nature, the superiority of a man to the accidents of a man.... On earth only one thing he finds which is thoroughly venerable, and that is the nature of man; not the accidents, which make a man rich or famous, but the substance, which makes him a man. The man is before the institutions of man; his nature superior to his history. All finite things are only appendages of man, useful, convenient, or beautiful. Man is master, and nature his slave, serving for many a varied use. The results of human experience—the state, the church, society, the family, business, literature, science, art—all of these are subordinate to man: if they serve the individual, he is to foster them, if not, to abandon them and seek better things. He looks at all things, the past and the present, the state and the church, Christianity and the market-house, in the daylight of the intellect. Nothing is allowed to stand between him and his manhood. Hence, there is an apparent irreverence; he does not bow to any hat . . . set up for public adoration, but to every man, canonical or profane, who bears the mark of native manliness.... While he is the most American, he is almost the most cosmopolitan of our writers, the least restrained and belittled by the popular follies of the nation or the age....

He spurns all constitutions but the law of his own nature, rejecting them with manly scorn....

Yet, with all this freedom, there is no wilful display of it. He is so confident of his freedom, so perfectly possessed of his rights, that he does not talk of them. They appear, but are not spoken of. With the hopefulness and buoyant liberty of America, he has none of our ill-mannered boasting....

While his Idea is American, the form of his literature is not less so. It is a form which suits the substance, and is modified by the institutions and natural objects about him. You see that the author lives in a land with free institutions, with town-meetings and ballot-boxes; ... He knows the humblebee, the blackbird, the bat, and the wren, and is not ashamed to say or sing of the things under his own eyes. He illustrates his high thought by common things out of our plain New England life—the meeting in the church, the Sunday school, the dancing-school, a huckleberry party, . . . —and out of all these he makes his poetry, or illustrates his philosophy. . . .

In his reading and his study, he is still his own master. He has not purchased his education with the loss of his identity, not of his manhood; nay, he has not forgotten his kindred in getting his culture. He is still the master of himself; no man provokes him even into a momentary imitation. . . . His style is allusive, . . . and the allusions are to literature which is known to but few. Hence, while his thought is human in substance, and American in its modifications, and therefore easily grasped, comprehended, and welcomed by men of the commonest culture, it is but few who understand the entire meaning of the sentences which he writes. His style reflects American scenery, and is dimpled into rare beauty as it flows by, and so has a pleasing fascination, but it reflects also the literary scenery of his own mind, and so half of his thought is lost on half his readers. . . .

Emerson's works do not betray any exact scholarship, which has a certain totality, as well as method about it. It is plain to see that his favorite authors have been Plutarch, . . . Montaigne, Shakspeare, George Herbert, Milton, Wordsworth, Coleridge, and Carlyle. Of late years, his works contain allusions to the ancient oriental literature, from which he has borrowed some hard names and some valuable thoughts, but is occasionally led astray by its influence, for it is plain that he does not understand that curious philosophy he quotes from. Hence his oriental allies are brought up to take a stand which no man dreamed of in their time . . .

In Emerson's writings, you do not see indications of exact mental discipline . . . He works up scientific facts in his writings with great skill, often penetrating beyond the fact, and discussing the idea out of which it, and many other kindred facts seem to have proceeded: this indicates not only a nice eye for facts, but a mind singularly powerful to detect latent analogies, and see the one in the many. Yet there is nothing to show any regular and systematic discipline in science . . .

With all his literary culture he has an intense love of nature, a true sight and appreciation thereof; not the analytic eye of the naturalist, but the synthetic vision of the poet. . . .

Mr. Emerson's writings are eminently religious; christian in the best sense of that word. This has often been denied for two reasons: because Mr. Emerson sets little value on the mythology of the Christian sects, . . . and also because his writings far transcend the mechanical morality and formal pietism, commonly recommended by gentlemen in pulpits. Highly religious, he is not at all ecclesiastical or bigoted. He has small reverence for forms and traditions; a manly life is the only form of religion which he recognizes, and hence we do not wonder at all that he also has been deemed an infidel. . . . Still it is not religion that is most conspicuous in these volumes . . .

To show what is in Mr. Emerson's books and what is not, let us make a little more detailed examination thereof. He is not a logical writer, not systematic; not what is commonly called philosophical; didactic to a great degree, but never demonstrative. So we are not to look for a scientific plan, or for a system, of which the author is himself conscious. . . .

Most writers, knowingly or unconsciously, take as their point of departure some special and finite thing. . . .

Mr. Emerson takes Man for his point of departure, he means to take the whole of man; man with his history, man with his nature, his sensational, intellectual, moral, affectional and religious instincts and faculties. With him man is the measure of all things, of ideas and of facts; if they fit man they are accepted, if not, thrown aside. . . .

In this Emerson is more American than America herself—and is himself the highest exponent in literature of this Idea of human freedom and the value of man. . . . Still we think it is not the whole of man from which he starts, that he undervalues the logical, demonstrative and historical Understanding, with the results thereof, and also undervalues the Affections. Hence his Man, who is the measure of all things, is not the complete man. This defect appears in his ethics, which are a little cold, the ethics of marble men; and in his religious teachings, the highest which this age has furnished, full of reverence, full of faith, but not proportionably rich in affection.

Mr. Emerson has a method of his own . . . rigidly adhered to. It is not the inductive method by which you arrive at a general fact from many particular facts, but never reach a universal law; it is not the deductive method, whereby a minor law is derived from a major, a special from a general law; it is neither inductive nor deductive demonstration. But Emerson proceeds by the way of intuition, sensational or spiritual. Go to the fact and look for yourself, is his command: a material fact you cannot always verify, and so for that must depend on evidence; a spiritual fact you can always legitimate for yourself. . . .

He is sometimes extravagant in the claims made for his own method, and maintains that ecstasy is the natural and exclusive mode of arriving at new truths, while it is only one mode. Ecstasy is the state of intuition in which the man loses his individual self-consciousness. . . .

Mr. Emerson says books are only for one's idle hours; he discourages hard and continuous thought, conscious modes of argument, of discipline. Here he exaggerates his idiosyncracy into a universal law. The method of nature is not ecstasy but patient attention. Human nature avenges herself for the slight he puts on her, by the irregular and rambling character of his own productions. . . .

In all Emerson's works there appears a sublime confidence in man; a respect for human nature which we have never seen surpassed—never equalled. Man is only to be true to his nature, to plant himself on his instincts, and all will turn out well . . .

He has also an absolute confidence in God. He has been foolishly accused of pantheism which sinks God in nature; but no man is further from it. He never sinks God in man, he does not stop with the law, in matter or morals, but goes back to the Lawgiver ... With this confidence in God he looks things fairly in the face, and never dodges, never fears. Toil, sorrow, pain, these are things which it is impious to fear. Boldly he faces every fact, never retreating behind an institution or a great man. In God his trust is complete; with the severest scrutiny he joins the highest reverence.

Hence come his calmness and serenity. He is evenly balanced and at repose. A more tranquil spirit cannot be found in literature. . . .

With the exceptions above stated, there is a remarkable balance of intellectual faculties, of creative and conservative, of the spontaneous and intuitive, and the voluntary and reflective powers. . . . If we go a little further and inquire how the other qualities are blended with the intellectual, we find that the moral power a little outweighs the intellectual, and the religious is a little before the moral, as it should be, but the affections seem to be less developed than the intellect. There is no total balance of all the faculties to correspond with the harmony of his intellectual powers. This seems to us the greatest defect in his entire being, as lack of logical power is the chief defect in his intellect; there is love enough for almost any man—not enough to balance his intellect, his conscience, and his faith in God. Hence there appears a certain coldness in his ethics. . . . Notwithstanding his own intense individuality and his theoretic and practical respect for individuality, still persons seem of small value to him—of little value except as they represent or help develop an idea of the intellect. In this respect, in his writings he is one-sided, and while no one mental power has subdued another, yet his intellect and conscience seem to enslave and belittle the affections. . . .

Let us now say a word of the artistic style and rhetorical form of these remarkable books. Mr. Emerson always gravitates towards first principles, but never sets them in a row, groups them into a system, or makes of them a whole. Hence the form of all his prose writings is very defective and much of his rare power is lost. . . . His separate thoughts are each a growth. Now and then it is so with a sentence, seldom with a paragraph; but his essay is always a piece of composition, carpentry, and not growth. . . .

In each essay there is the same want of organic completeness and orderly distribution of the parts. There is no logical arrangement of the separate thoughts, which are subordinate to the main idea of the piece. They are shot together into a curious and disorderly mass of beauty . . . Towards the end the interest deepens, not from an artistic arrangement of accumulated thoughts, but only because the author finds his heart warmed by his efforts, and beating quicker. . . .

His marked love of individuality appears in his style. His thoughts are seldom vague, all is distinct; the outlines sharply drawn, things are always discrete from one another. He loves to particularize. He talks not of flowers, but of the violet, the clover . . . It is remarkable to what an extent this individualization is carried. The essays in his books are separate and stand apart from one another, only mechanically bound by the lids of the volume; his paragraphs in each essay are distinct and disconnected, or but loosely bound to one another; it is so with sentences in the paragraph, and propositions in the sentence. . . . But this very lack of order gives variety of form. You can never anticipate him. . . .

His style is one of the rarest beauty; there is no affectation, no conceit, no effort at effect. He alludes to everybody and imitates nobody. . . . Emerson builds a rambling Gothic Church, with an irregular outline, a chapel here, and a tower there, you do not see why; but all parts are beautiful and the whole constrains the soul to love and trust. . . .

From what has been said, notwithstanding the faults we have found in Emerson, it is plain that we assign him a very high rank in the literature of mankind. He is a very extraordinary man. To no English writer since Milton can we assign so high a place; . . . Emerson is a man of genius such as does not often appear, such as has never appeared before in America, and but seldom in the world. He learns from all sorts of men, but no English writer, we think, is so original. We sincerely lament the want of logic in his method, and his exaggeration of the intuitive powers . . . In Emerson's poetry there is often a ruggedness and want of finish which seems wilful in a man like him. . . . Spite of these defects, Mr. Emerson, on the whole, speaks with a holy power which no other man possesses who now writes the English tongue. . . .

This is his source of strength: his intellectual and moral sincerity. He looks after Truth, Justice, and Beauty. He has not uttered a word that is false to his own mind or conscience; has not suppressed a word because he thought it too high for men's comprehension, and therefore dangerous to the repose of men. . . .

He has not written a line which is not conceived in the interest of mankind. He never writes in the interest of a section, of a party, of a church, of a man, always in the interest of mankind. Hence comes the ennobling influence of his works. . . . Emerson belongs to the exceptional literature of the times—and while his culture joins him to the history of man, his ideas and his whole life enable him to represent also the nature of man, and so to write for the future.

From "The Writings of Ralph Waldo Emerson," *The Massachusetts Quarterly Review* (Boston), 3 (March 1850), 200-255.

HENRY JAMES, JR.

THIS LITTLE epoch of fermentation [Boston transcendentalism] has three or four drawbacks for the critics—drawbacks, however, that may be overlooked by a person for whom it has an interest of association. It bore, intellectually, the stamp of provincialism; it was a beginning without a fruition, a dawn without a noon; and it produced, with a single exception, no great talents. It produced a great deal of writing, but . . . only one writer in whom the world at large has interested itself. The situation was summed up and transfigured in the admirable and exquisite Emerson. He expressed all that it contained, and a good deal more, doubtless, besides; he was the man of genius of the moment; he was the Transcendentalist *par excellence*. Emerson expressed, before all things, as was extremely natural at the hour and in the place, the value and importance of the individual, the duty of making the most of one's self, of living by one's own personal light, and carrying out one's own disposition. He reflected with beautiful irony upon the exquisite impudence of those institutions which claim to have appropriated the truth and to dole it out, in proportionate morsels, in exchange for a subscription. He talked about the beauty and dignity of life, and about every one who is born into the world being born to the whole, having an interest and a stake in the whole. He said "all that is clearly due to-day is not to lie," and a great many other things which it would be still easier to present in a ridiculous light. He insisted upon sincerity and independence and spontaneity, upon acting in harmony with one's nature, and not conforming and compromising for the sake of being more comfortable. He urged that a man should await his call, his finding the thing to do which he should really believe in doing, and not be urged by the world's opinion to do simply the world's work. "If no call should come for years, for centuries, then I know that the want of the Universe is the attestation of faith by my abstinence. . . . If I cannot work, at least I need not lie." The doctrine of the supremacy of the individual to himself, of his originality, and, as regards his own character, *unique* quality, must have had a great charm for people living in a society in which introspection—thanks to the want of other entertainment—played almost the part of a social resource.

In the United States, in those days, there were no great things to look out at (save forests and rivers); life was not in the least spectacular;

society was not brilliant; the country was given up to a great material prosperity, a homely *bourgeois* activity, a diffusion of primary education and the common luxuries. There was, therefore, among the cultivated classes, much relish for the utterances of a writer who would help one to take a picturesque view of one's internal responsibilities, and to find in the landscape of the soul all sorts of fine sunrise and moonlight effects. "Meantime, while the doors of the temple stand open, night and day, before every man, and the oracles of this truth cease never, it is guarded by one stern condition; this, namely—it is an intuition. It cannot be received at second hand. Truly speaking, it is not instruction but provocation that I can receive from another soul." To make one's self so much more interesting would help to make life interesting, and life was probably, to many of this aspiring congregation, a dream of freedom and fortitude. There were faulty parts in the Emersonian philosophy; but the general tone was magnificent; and I can easily believe that, coming when it did and where it did, it should have been drunk in by a great many fine moral appetites with a sense of intoxication. One envies, even, I will not say the illusions, of that keenly sentient period, but the convictions and interests—the moral passion. One certainly envies the privilege of having heard the finest of Emerson's orations poured forth in their early newness. They were the most poetical, the most beautiful productions of the American mind, and they were thoroughly local and national. They had a music and a magic, and when one remembers the remarkable charm of the speaker, the beautiful modulation of his utterance, one regrets in especial that one might not have been present on a certain occasion which made a sensation, an era—the delivery of an address to the Divinity School of Harvard University, on a summer evening in 1838. In the light, fresh American air, unthickened and undarkened by customs and institutions established, these things, as the phrase is, told.

From *Hawthorne* (New York: Harper & Brothers, 1879), pp. 81-84.

MATTHEW ARNOLD

MILTON SAYS that poetry ought to be simple, sensuous, impassioned. Well, Emerson's poetry is seldom either simple, or sensuous, or impassioned. In general it lacks directness; it lacks concreteness; it lacks energy. His grammar is often embarrassed; in particular, the want of clearly-marked distinction between the subject and the object of his sentence is a frequent cause of obscurity in him. A poem which shall be a plain, forcible, inevitable whole he hardly ever produces. Such good work as the noble lines graven on the Concord Monument is the exception with him; such ineffective work as the 'Fourth of July Ode' or the 'Boston Hymn' is the rule. Even passages and single lines of thorough plainness and commanding force are rare in his poetry. They exist, of course; but when we meet with them they give us a slight shock of surprise, so little has Emerson accustomed us to them. Let me have the pleasure of quoting one or two of these exceptional passages:—

'So nigh is grandeur to our dust,
    So near is God to man,
When Duty whispers low, *Thou must,*
    The youth replies, *I can.*'

Or again this:—

'Though love repine and reason chafe,
There came a voice without reply:
" 'Tis man's perdition to be safe,
When for the truth he ought to die."

Excellent! but how seldom do we get from him a strain blown so clearly and firmly! Take another passage where his strain has not only clearness, it has also grace and beauty:—

'And ever, when the happy child
In May beholds the blooming wild,
And hears in heaven the bluebird sing,
"Onward," he cries, "your baskets bring!
In the next field is air more mild,
And in yon hazy west is Eden's balmier
    spring." '

In the style and cadence here there is a reminiscence, I think, of Gray; at any rate the pureness, grace, and beauty of these lines are worthy even of Gray. But Gray holds his high rank as a poet, not merely by the beauty and grace of passages in his poems; not merely by a diction generally pure in an age of impure diction: he holds it, above all, by the power and skill with which the evolution of his poems is conducted. . . . Emerson's 'Mayday,' from which I just now quoted, has no real evolution at all; it is a series of observations. And, in general, his poems have no evolution. Take, for example, his 'Titmouse.' Here he has an excellent subject; and his observation of Nature, moreover, is always marvellously close and fine. But compare what he makes of his meeting with his titmouse with what Cowper or Burns makes of the like kind of incident! One never quite arrives at learning what the titmouse actually did for him at all, though one feels a strong interest and desire to learn it; but one is reduced to guessing, and cannot be quite sure that after all one has guessed right. He is not plain and concrete enough,—in other words, not poet enough,—to be able to tell us. And a failure of this kind goes through almost all his verse, keeps him amid symbolism and allusion and the fringes of things, and, in spite of his spiritual power, deeply impairs his poetic value. . . .

I do not, then, place Emerson among the great poets. But I go further, and say that I do not place him among the great writers, the great men of letters. Who are the great men of letters? They are men like Cicero, Plato, Bacon, Pascal, Swift, Voltaire,—writers with, in the first place, a genius and instinct for style; writers whose prose is by a kind of native necessity true and sound. Now the style of Emerson, like the style of his transcendentalist friends and of the 'Dial' so continually,—the style of Emerson is capable of falling into a strain like this, which I take from the beginning of his 'Essay on Love': 'Every soul is a celestial being to every other soul. The heart has its sabbaths and jubilees, in which the world appears as a hymeneal feast, and all natural sounds and the circle of the seasons are erotic odes and dances.' Emerson altered this sentence in the later editions. Like Wordsworth, he was in later life fond of altering; and in general his later alterations, like those of Wordsworth, are not improvements. He softened the passage in question, however, though without really mending it. I quote it in its original and strongly-marked form. . . . Unsound it is, indeed, and in a style almost impossible to a born man of letters.

It is a curious thing, that quality of style which marks the great writer, the born man of letters. It resides in the whole tissue of his work, and of his work regarded as a composition for literary purposes. Brilliant and powerful passages in a man's writings do not prove his possession of it; it lies in their whole tissue. Emerson has passages of noble and pathetic eloquence . . . ; he has passages of shrewd and felicitous wit; he has crisp epigram; he has passages of exquisitely touched observation of nature. Yet he is not a great writer; his style has not the requisite wholeness of good tissue. . . .

You will think I deal in nothing but negatives. I have been saying that Emerson is not one of the great poets, the great writers. He has not their quality of style. He is, however, the propounder of a philosophy. . . . Emerson cannot, I think, be called with justice a great philosophical writer. He cannot build; his arrangement of philosophical ideas has no progress in it, no evolution; he does not construct a philosophy. Emerson himself knew the defects of his method, or rather want of method, very well; indeed, he and Carlyle criticise themselves and one another in a way which leaves little for any one else to do in the way of formulating their defects. . . .

Some people will tell you that Emerson's poetry, indeed, is too abstract, and his philosophy too vague, but that his best work is his *English Traits*. The *English Traits* are beyond question very pleasant reading. It is easy to praise them, easy to commend the author of them. But I insist on always trying Emerson's work by the highest standards. I esteem him too much to try his work by any other. Tried by the highest standards, and compared with the work of the excellent markers and recorders of the traits of human life,—of writers like Montaigne, La Bruyère, Addison,—the *English Traits* will not stand the comparison. Emerson's observation has not the disinterested quality of the observation of these masters. It is the observation of a man systematically benevolent . . . Emerson's systematic benevolence comes from what he himself calls somewhere his 'persistent optimism'; and his persistent optimism is the root of his greatness and the source of his charm. But still let us keep our literary conscience true, and judge every kind of literary work by the laws really proper to it. The kind of work attempted in the *English Traits* . . . is work which cannɔt be done perfectly with a bias such as that given by Emerson's optimism . . .

We have not in Emerson a great poet, a great writer, a great philosophy-maker. His relation to us is not that of one of those personages; yet it is a relation of, I think, even superior importance. His relation to us is more like that of the Roman Emperor Marcus Aurelius. Marcus Aurelius is not a great writer, a great philosophy-maker; he is the friend and aider of those who would live in the spirit. Emerson is the same. He is the friend and aider of those who would live in the spirit. All the points in thinking which are necessary for this purpose he takes; but he does not combine them into a system, or present them as a regular philosophy. Combined in a system by a man with the requisite talent for this kind of thing, they would be less useful than as Emerson gives them to us; and the man with the talent so to systematise them would be less impressive than Emerson. They do very well as they now stand;

—like 'boulders,' as he says;—in 'paragraphs incompressible, each sentence an infinitely repellent particle.' In such sentences his main points recur again and again, and become fixed in the memory. . . .

This [Emerson's law of compensation] is tonic indeed! And let no one object that it is too general; that more practical, positive direction is what we want; that Emerson's optimism, self-reliance, and indifference to favourable conditions for our life and growth have in them something of danger. . . . In the New England, as in the Old, our people have to learn, I suppose, not that their modes of life are beautiful and excellent already; they have rather to learn that they must transform them.

To adopt this line of objection to Emerson's deliverances would, however, be unjust. In the first place, Emerson's points are in themselves true, if understood in a certain high sense; they are true and fruitful. And the right work to be done, at the hour when he appeared, was to affirm them generally and absolutely. Only thus could he break through the hard and fast barrier of narrow, fixed ideas, which he found confronting him, and win an entrance for new ideas. Had he attempted developments which may now strike us as expedient, he would have excited fierce antagonism, and probably effected little or nothing. The time might come for doing other work later, but the work which Emerson did was the right work to be done then.

In the second place, strong as was Emerson's optimism, and unconquerable as was his belief in a good result to emerge from all which he saw going on around him, no misanthropical satirist ever saw shortcomings and absurdities more clearly than he did, or exposed them more courageously. When he sees 'the meanness,' as he calls it, 'of American politics,' he congratulates Washington on being 'long already happily dead,' on being 'wrapt in his shroud and for ever safe.' With how firm a touch he delineates the faults of your two great political parties of forty years ago! . . . 'From neither party, when in power, has the world any benefit to expect in science, art, or humanity, at all commensurate with the resources of the nation.' Then with what subtle though kindly irony he follows the gradual withdrawal in New England, in the last half century, of tender consciences from the social organisations,—the bent for experiments such as that of Brook Farm and the like,—follows it in all its 'dissidence of dissent and Protestantism of the Protestant religion!' He even loves to rally the New Englander on his philanthropical activity, and to find his beneficence and its institutions a bore! . . .

Yes, truly, his insight is admirable; his truth is precious. Yet the secret of his effect is not even in these; it is in his temper. It is in the hopeful, serene, beautiful temper wherewith these, in Emerson, are indissolubly joined; in which they work, and have their being. He says himself: 'We judge of a man's wisdom by his hope, knowing that the perception of the inexhaustibleness of nature is an immortal youth.' If this be so, how wise is Emerson! for never had man such a sense of the inexhaustibleness of nature, and such hope. It was the ground of his being; it never failed him. Even when he is sadly avowing the imperfection of his literary power and resources, lamenting his fumbling fingers and stammering tongue, he adds: 'Yet, as I tell you, I am very easy in my mind and never dream of suicide. My whole philosophy, which is very real, teaches acquiescence and optimism. Sure I am that the right word will be spoken, though I cut out my tongue.' In his old age, with friends dying and life failing, his tone of cheerful, forward-looking hope is still the same. . . .

One can scarcely overrate the importance of thus holding fast to happiness and hope. It gives to Emerson's work an invaluable virtue. As Wordsworth's poetry is, in my judgment, the most important work done in verse, in our language, during the present century, so Emerson's *Essays* are, I think, the most important work done in prose. . . .

Happiness in labour, righteousness, and veracity; in all the life of the spirit; happiness and eternal hope;—that was Emerson's gospel. I hear it said that Emerson was too sanguine; that the actual generation in America is not turning out so well as he expected. Very likely he was too sanguine as to the near future; in this country it is difficult not to be too sanguine. Very possibly the present generation may prove unworthy of his high hopes; even several generations succeeding this may prove unworthy of them. But by his conviction that in the life of the spirit is happiness, and by his hope that this life of the spirit will come more and more to be sanely understood, and to prevail, and to work for happiness,—by this conviction and hope Emerson was great, and he will surely prove in the end to have been right in them.

From "Emerson" in *Discourses in America* (New York: Macmillan, 1906), pp. 138-207—originally published in 1885 from a lecture given during Arnold's "triumphal tour" in the United States in 1883-84.

OLIVER WENDELL HOLMES

TOO MUCH has been made of Emerson's mysticism. He was an intellectual rather than an emotional mystic, and withal a cautious one. He never let go the string of his balloon. He never threw over all his ballast of common sense so as to rise above an atmosphere in which a rational being could breathe. I found in his library William Law's edition of Jacob Behmen. There were all those wonderful diagrams over which the reader may have grown dizzy,—just such as one finds on the walls of lunatic asylums,—evidences to all sane minds of cerebral strabismus in the contrivers of them. Emerson liked to lose himself for a little while in the vagaries of this class of minds, the dangerous proximity of which to insanity he knew and has spoken of. He played with the incommunicable, the inconceivable, the absolute, the antinomies, as he would have played with a bundle of jackstraws. "Brahma," the poem which so mystified the readers of the "Atlantic Monthly," was one of his spiritual divertisements. To the average Western mind it is the nearest approach to a Torricellian vacuum of intelligibility that language can pump out of itself. . . .

Of course no one can hold Emerson responsible for the "Yoga" doctrine of Brahmanism, which he has amused himself with putting in verse. The oriental side of Emerson's nature delighted itself in these narcotic dreams, born in the land of the poppy and of hashish. They lend a peculiar charm to his poems, but it is not worth while to try to construct a philosophy out of them. The knowledge, if knowledge it be, of the mystic is not transmissible. It is not cumulative; it begins and ends with the solitary dreamer, and the next who follows him has to build his own cloud-castle as if it were the first aerial edifice that a human soul had ever constructed.

Some passages of "Nature," "The Over-Soul," "The Sphinx," "Uriel," illustrate sufficiently this mood of spiritual exaltation. Emerson's calm temperament never allowed it to reach the condition he sometimes refers to,—that of ecstasy. The passage in "Nature" where he says "I become a transparent eyeball" is about as near it as he ever came. This was almost too much for some of his admirers and worshippers. . . .

Emerson's reflections in the "transcendental" mood do beyond question sometimes irresistibly suggest the close neighborhood of the sublime to the ridiculous. But very near that precipitous border line there is a charmed region where, if the statelier growths of philosophy die out and disappear, the flowers of poetry next the very edge of the chasm have a peculiar and mysterious beauty. "Uriel" is a poem which finds itself perilously near to the gulf of unsounded obscurity, and has, I doubt not, provoked the mirth of profane readers; but read in a lucid moment, it is just obscure enough and just significant enough to give the voltaic thrill which comes from the sudden contacts of the highest imaginative conceptions.

Human personality presented itself to Emerson as a passing phase of universal being. Born of the Infinite, to the Infinite it was to return. Sometimes he treats his own personality as interchangeable with objects in nature,—he would put it off like a garment and clothe himself in the landscape. Here is a curious extract from "The Adirondacs," . . .

> "And presently the sky is changed; O world!
> What pictures and what harmonies are thine!
> The clouds are rich and dark, the air serene,
> *So like the soul of me, what if't were me?*"

We find this idea of confused personal identity also in a brief poem printed among the "Translations" in the second part of Emerson's Poems. These are the last two lines of "The Flute, from Hilali":—

> "Saying, Sweetheart! the old mystery remains,
> If I am I; thou, thou, or thou art I? " . . .

Once more, how fearfully near the abyss of the ridiculous! A few drops of alcohol bring about a confusion of mind not unlike this poetical metempsychosis. . . .

I have not lost my reverence for Emerson in showing one of his fancies for a moment in the distorting mirror of the ridiculous. He would doubtless have smiled with me at the reflection, for he had a keen sense of humor. . . .

The mystic appeals to those only who have an ear for the celestial concords, as the musician only appeals to those who have the special endowment which enables them to understand his compositions. It is not for organizations untuned to earthly music to criticise the great composers, or for those who are deaf to spiritual harmonies to criticise the higher natures which lose themselves in the strains of divine contemplation. . . .

Emerson's style is epigrammatic, incisive, authoritative, sometimes quaint, never obscure, except when he is handling nebulous subjects. His paragraphs are full of brittle sentences that break apart and are independent units, like the fragments of a coral colony. His imagery is frequently daring, leaping from the concrete to the abstract, from the special to the general and universal, and *vice versa*, with a bound that is like a flight. . . .

He is fond of certain archaisms and unusual phrases. He likes the expression "mother-wit," which he finds in Spenser, Marlowe, Shakespeare, and other old writers. He often uses the word "husband" in its earlier sense of economist. His use of the word "haughty" is so fitting, and it sounds so nobly from his lips, that we could wish its employment were forbidden henceforth to voices which vulgarize it. But his special, constitutional, word is "fine," meaning something like dainty, as Shakespeare uses it,—"my dainty Ariel,"—"fine Ariel." It belongs to his habit of mind and body . . . "Melioration" is another favorite word of Emerson's. A clairvoyant could spell out some of his most characteristic traits by the aid of his use of these three words; his inborn fastidiousness, subdued and kept out of sight by his large charity and his good breeding, showed itself in his liking for the word "haughty;" his exquisite delicacy by his fondness for the word "fine," with a certain shade of meaning; his optimism in the frequent recurrence of the word "melioration."

We must not find fault with his semi-detached sentences until we quarrel with Solomon and criticise the Sermon on the Mount. The "point and surprise" which he speaks of as characterizing the style of Plutarch belong eminently to his own. His fertility of illustrative imagery is very great. His images are noble, or, if borrowed from humble objects, ennobled by his handling. He throws his royal robe over a milking-stool and it becomes a throne. But chiefly he chooses objects of comparison grand in themselves. He deals with the elements at first hand. Such delicacy of treatment, with such breadth and force of effect, is hard to match anywhere, and we know him by his style at sight. . . . We have seen him as an unpretending lecturer. We follow him round as he "peddles out all the wit he can gather from Time or from Nature," and we find that "he has changed his market cart into a chariot of the sun," and is carrying about the morning light as merchandise.

From *Ralph Waldo Emerson* (Boston: Houghton, Mifflin, 1884), pp. 396-406.

EDMUND CLARENCE STEDMAN

IN HIS VERSE, Emerson's spiritual philosophy and laws of conduct appear again, but transfigured. Always the idea of Soul, central and pervading, of which Nature's forms are but the created symbols. As in his early discourse he recognized two entities, Nature and the Soul, so to the last he believed Art to be simply the union of Nature with man's will—Thought symbolizing itself through Nature's aid. Thought, sheer ideality, was his sovereign; he was utterly trustful of its guidance. The law of poetic beauty depends on the beauty of the thought, which, perforce, assumes the fittest, and therefore most charming, mode of expression. The key to art is the eternal fitness of things; this is the sure test and solvent. Over and again he asserted his conviction: "Great thoughts insure musical expression. Every word should be the right word. . . . The Imagination wakened brings its own language, and that is always musical. . . . Whatever language the poet uses, the secret of tone is at the heart of the poem." He cites Möller, who taught that the building which was fitted accurately to answer its end would turn out to be beautiful, though beauty had not been intended. . . . In fine, Emerson sees all forms of art symbolizing but one Reason, not one mind, but The Mind that made the world. He refers "all production at last to an aboriginal Power." It is easy to discern that from the first he recognized "the motion and the spirit," which to Wordsworth were revealed only by the discipline of years; but his song went beyond the range of landscape and peasant, touching upon the verities of life and thought. "Brahma" is the presentation of the truth manifest to the oldest and most eastern East, and beyond which the West can never go. How strange that these quatrains could have seemed strange! They reveal the light of Asia, but no less the thought of Plato—who said that in all nations certain minds dwell on the "fundamental Unity," and "lose all being in one Being." Everywhere one stuff, under all forms, this the woven symbolism of the universal Soul, the only reality, the single and subdivided Identity that alone can "keep and pass and turn again," that is at once the doubter and the doubt, the slayer and the slain, light and shadow, the hither and the yon. Love is but the affinity of its portions, the desire for reunion, the knowledge of soul by soul, to which the eyes of lovers are but windows. Art is the handiwork of the soul, with materials created by itself, building better than it knows, the bloom of attraction and necessity.

Thus far the theory of Emerson's song. It does not follow that he composed upon a theory. At times I think him the first of our lyric poets, his turns are so wild and unexpected; and he was never commonplace, even when writing for occasions. His verse changes unawares from a certain tension and angularity that were congenital, to an ethereal, unhampered freedom, the poetic soul in full glow, the inner music loosed and set at large. . . . Emerson made philosophical poetry imaginative, elevating, and thus gave new evidence that the poet's realm is unbounded. If he sought first principles, he looked within himself for them, and thus portrays himself, not only the penetrative thinker, but the living man, the citizen, the New England villager, whose symbols are drawn from the actual woods and hills of a neighborhood. Certainly he went to rural nature for his vigor, his imagery and adornments. An impassioned sense of its beauty made him the reverse of the traditional descriptive poet. . . .

"Woodnotes" is full of lyrical ecstasy and lightsome turns and graces. To assimilate such a poem of nature, or "The Problem," that masterpiece of religion and art, is to feed on holy dew, and to comprehend how the neophytes who were bred upon it find the manna of noontide somewhat rank and innutritious. "May-Day" is less lyrical, more plainly descriptive of the growth and meaning of the Spring, but not in any part didactic. It is the record of the poet's training, a match to Wordsworth's portrayal of his subjective communing with Nature in youth; its spirit is the same with Lowell's woodland joyousness, one of child-like and unquestioning zest. Finally, this poet's scenic joinery is so true, so mortised with the one apt word, as where he says that the wings of Time are "*pied* with morning and with night," and the one best word or phrase is so unlooked for, that, as I say, we scarcely know whether all this comes by grace of instinct, or with search and artistic forethought. . . . His generalizations pertain to the unseen world; viewing the actual, he puts its strength and fineness alike into a line or epithet. He was born with an unrivalled faculty of selection. Monadnock is the "constant giver," the Titan that "heeds his sky-affairs"; the tiny humming-bee a "voyager of light and noon," a "yellow-breeched philosopher," and again an "animated torrid zone"; the defiant titmouse, an "atom in full breath." For a snow-storm, or the ocean, he uses his broader brush, but once only and well. . . .

Thus keenly Emerson's instinct responded to the beauty of Nature. I have hinted that her secure laws were the chief promoters of his imagination. It coursed along her hidden ways. In this he antedated Tennyson, and was less didactic than Goethe and kindred predecessors. His foresight gave spurs to the intellect of Tyndall and other investigators,—to their ideal faculty, without which no explorer moves from post to outpost of discovery. Correlatively, each wonder-breeding point attained by the experimentalists was also occupied by our eager and learned thinker from the moment of its certainty. Each certainty gave him joy; reasoning *a priori* from his sense of a spiritual Force, the seer anticipated the truths demonstrated by the inductive workers, and expected the demonstration. Even in "The Sphinx," the first poem of his first collection, the conservation of force, the evolution from the primordial atom, are made to subserve his mystical faith in a broad Identity. . . .

It should be noted that Emerson's vision of the sublime in scientific discovery increased his distaste for mere style, and moved him to contentment with the readiest mode of expression. It tempered his eulogy of "Art," and made him draw this contrast: "Nature transcends all moods of thought, and its secret we do not yet find. But a gallery stands at the mercy of our moods, and there is a moment when it becomes frivolous. I do not wonder that Newton, with an attention habitually engaged on the paths of planets and suns, should have wondered what the Earl of Pembroke found to admire in 'stone dolls.' "

Right here we observe (deferring matters of construction) that our seer's limitations as a poet are indicated by his dependence on out-door nature, and by his failure to utilize those higher symbols of the prime Intelligence which comprise the living, acting, suffering world of man. With a certain pride of reserve, that did not lessen his beautiful deference to individuals, he proclaimed "the advantage which the country life possesses for a powerful mind over the artificial and curtailed life of cities." He justified solitude by saying that great men, from Plato to Wordsworth, did not live in a crowd, but descended into it from time to time as benefactors. Above all he declared—"I am by nature a poet, and therefore must live in the country." But here a Goethe, or De Musset, or Browning might rejoin: "And I am a poet, and need the focal life of the town." If man be the paragon of life on this globe, his works and passions the rarest symbols of the life unseen, then the profoundest study is mankind. Emerson's theorem was a restriction of the poet's liberties. One can name great poets who would have been greater but for the trammels of their seclusion. I believe that Emerson's came from self-knowledge. He kept his range with incomparable tact and philosophy. Poets of a wider franchise—with Shakespeare at their front—have found that genius gains most from Nature during that formative period when one reads her heart, if ever, and that afterward he may safely leave her, as a child his mother, to return from time to time, but still to do his part among the ranks of men.

Emerson makes light of travel for pleasure and observation, but ever more closely would observe the ways of the inanimate world. Yet what are man's works but the works of Nature by one remove? To one poet is given the ear to comprehend the murmur of the forest, to another the sense that times the heartbeats of humanity. Few have had Emerson's inward eye, but it is well that some have not been restricted to it. . . .

His verse, in fact, is almost wholly void of the epic and dramatic elements which inform the world's great works of art. Action, characterization, specific sympathy, and passion are wanting in his song. His voice comes "like a falling star" from a skyey dome of pure abstraction. Once or twice, some little picture from life,—a gypsy girl, a scarcely outlined friend or loved one,—but otherwise no personage in his works except, it may be, the poet himself, . . . Emerson would be the "best bard, because the wisest," if the wisdom of his song illustrated itself in living types. He knew the human world, none better, and generalized the sum of its attainments,—was gracious, shrewd, and calm,—but could not hold up the mirror and show us to ourselves. He was that unique songster, a poet of fire and vision, quite above the moralist, yet neither to be classed as objective or subjective; he perceived the source of all passion and wisdom, yet rendered neither the hearts of others nor his own. His love poetry is eulogized, but it wants the vital grip wherewith his "Concord Fight" and "Boston Hymn" fasten on our sense of manhood and patriotism. It chants of Love, not of the beloved; its flame is pure and general as moonlight and as high-removed. "All mankind love a lover," and it is not enough to discourse upon the philosophy of "Love," "Experience," "Power," "Friendship." Emerson's "Bacchus" must press for him

> ——"wine, but wine which never grew
> In the belly of the grape."

His deepest yearnings are expressed in that passionate outburst,—the momentary human wail over his dead child,—and in the human sense of lost companionship when he tells us,—

> "In the long sunny afternoon,
> The plain was full of ghosts."

Oftener he moves apart; his blood is ichor, not our own; his thoughts are with the firmament. We reverence his vocation, and know ourselves unfitted for it. He touches life more nearly in passages that have the acuteness, the practical wisdom of his prose works and days; but these are not his testimonials as a poet. . . .

The technical features of Emerson's verse correspond to our idea of its meaning. . . . Delicate and adroit artisans, in whose eyes poetry is solely a piece of design, may find the awkwardness of Emerson's verse a bar to right comprehension of its frequent beauty and universal purpose. I am not sure but one must be of the poet's own country and breeding to look quite down his vistas and by-paths . . . It may be, too, that other conditions are needed to open the ear to the melody, and to shut out the discords, of Emerson's song. The melody is there, and though the range be narrow, is various within itself. The charm is that of new-world and native wood-notes wild. Not seldom a lyrical phrase is the more taking for its halt,—helped out, like the poet's own speech, by the half-stammer and pause that were wont to precede the rarest or weightiest word of all . . . .

His greater efforts in verse, as in prose, show that he chose to deprecate the constructive faculty lest it might limit his ease and freedom. And his instinct of personality, not without a pride of its own, made him a nonconformist. . . . His early critic [Margaret Fuller] declared that he had not "written one good work, if such a work be one where the whole commands more attention than the parts." But again we see that she too rarely qualified her oracles. At that time he had written poems of which the whole and the parts were at least justly related masterpieces,—lyrical masterpieces, of course, not epic or dramatic; of such were the "Threnody" and "Woodnotes," to which was afterward added the "May-Day." Breadth and proportion, in a less degree, mark "The Problem," "Monadnock," "Merlin," and a few other pieces. But working similarly he falls short in the labored dithyrambic, "Initial, Daemonic, and Celestial Love." He was formal enough in youth, before he struck out for himself, and at the age of eleven, judging from his practice-work, was as precocious as Bryant or Poe. But he soon gave up construction, putting a trademark upon his verse, and trusting that freedom would lead to something new. So many precious sayings enrich his more sustained poems as to make us include him at times with the complete artists. Certainly, both in these and in the unique bits so characteristic that they are the poet himself,—"Terminus," "Character," "Manners," "Nature," etc.,—he ranks with the foremost of the second class, poets eminent for special graces, values, sudden meteors of thought. In that gift for "saying things," so notable in Pope and Tennyson, he is the chief of American poets. From what other bard have so many original lines and phrases passed into literature,—inscriptions that do not wear out, graven in bright and standard gold?

From *Poets of America* (Boston: Houghton Mifflin, 1885), pp. 133-79.

CHARLES J. WOODBURY

AN ORGANIC philosophy he did not offer. His claim was that there is nothing complete. The clement Parcae in his study, who were ever spinning a fairer thread, presided over his mental attitude, which always said, All objects are unknowable on account of their relativity. Nothing is concluded here or can be. I utter the final word on no subject. How different this from Beecher's study, for instance, where the great circular work-wheel and chair in the centre somehow always presented positive and final declaration. But Emerson would weave no completed fabric. Far be it from him to dogmatize or insist upon any pronouncement as complete or final. He said what he saw, and as far as he saw, without reasoning and without logical unfolding. Facts, yes: but let the reader do his own dreaming, and make his own completions. His reward does not depend on solidarity which is often artificial.

"Do not put hinges to your work to make it cohere," he once said in substance to me. And we must remember that through such joints much sophistry has crept into the world. Sincerity was Mr. Emerson's soul; and he unhesitatingly preferred lack of continuity to the least ambiguity regarding intention. Classification for the sake of external order and system was unnatural to him. Nor was he sensitive to their absence in Carlyle, whose writings are a congeries of magnificent contradictions. It may be that this temperament in Mr. Emerson asserted itself at times too strongly for his wish or his work, as certainly did his reluctance from severe thought. After his proposition had once attained form and been passed upon, it must remain. If the next could be made to harmonize with it, well; if not, the next must look out for itself; it, too, must be true, or it would not be here.

These omissions and silences in Emerson's literature reward, and it is well to master its cipher. It is the way a poet writes. Emerson was essentially a poet, and the essays are lyric and a solvent force. When even they discuss society it is with a poet's insight. No one reads them, any more than he would poetry, by quantity.

From *Talks with Ralph Waldo Emerson* (New York: Baker & Taylor, 1890), pp. 154-55.

JOHN JAY CHAPMAN

EMERSON REPRESENTS a protest against the tyranny of democracy. He is the most recent example of elemental hero-worship. His opinions are absolutely unqualified except by his temperament. He expresses a form of belief in the importance of the individual which is independent of any personal relations he has with the world. It is as if a man had been withdrawn from the earth and dedicated to condensing and embodying this eternal idea—the value of the individual soul—so vividly, so vitally, that his words could not die, yet in such illusive and abstract forms that by no chance and by no power could his creed be used for purposes of tyranny. Dogma cannot be extracted from it. Schools cannot be built on it. It either lives as the spirit lives, or else it evaporates and leaves nothing. Emerson was so afraid of the letter that killeth that he would hardly trust his words to print. He was assured there was no such thing as literal truth, but only literal falsehood. He therefore resorted to metaphors which could by no chance be taken literally. And he has probably succeeded in leaving a body of work which cannot be made to operate to any other end than that for which he designed it. If this be true, he has accomplished the inconceivable feat of eluding misconception. If it be true, he stands alone in the history of teachers; he has circumvented fate, he has left an unmixed blessing behind him.

The signs of those times which brought forth Emerson are not wholly undecipherable. They are the same times which gave rise to every character of significance during the period before the war. Emerson is indeed the easiest to understand of all the men of his time, because his life is freest from the tangles and qualifications of circumstance. He is a sheer and pure type and creature of destiny, and the unconsciousness that marks his development allies him to the deepest phenomena. It is convenient, in describing him, to use language which implies consciousness on his part, but he himself had no purpose, no theory of himself; he was a product. . . .

The generous youths who came to manhood between 1820 and 1830, while this deadly era [of limited individual freedom and subservience to opinion] was maturing, seem to have undergone a revulsion against the world almost before touching it; at least two of them suffered, revolted, and condemned, while still boys sitting on benches in school, and came forth advancing upon this old society like gladiators.

The activity of William Lloyd Garrison, the man of action, preceded by several years that of Emerson who is his prophet. Both of them were parts of one revolution. One of Emerson's articles of faith was that a man's thoughts spring from his actions rather than his actions from his thoughts, and possibly the same thing holds good for society at large. Perhaps all truths, whether moral or economic, must be worked out in real life before they are discovered by the student, and it was therefore necessary that Garrison should be evolved earlier than Emerson.

The silent years of early manhood, during which Emerson passed through the Divinity School and to his ministry, known by few, understood by none, least of all by himself, were years in which the revolting spirit of an archangel thought out his creed. He came forth perfect, with that serenity of which we have scarce another example in history, —that union of the man himself, his beliefs, and his vehicle of expression that makes men great because it makes them comprehensible. The [Platonic] philosophy into which he had already transmuted all his earlier theology at the time we first meet him consisted of a very simple drawing together of a few ideas, all of which had long been familiar to the world. It is the wonderful use he made of these ideas, the closeness with which they fitted his soul, the tact with which he took what he needed, like a bird building its nest, that make the originality, the man. . . .

His writings vary in coherence. In his early occasional pieces, like the Phi Beta Kappa address, coherence is at a maximum. They were written for a purpose, and were perhaps struck off all at once. But he earned his living by lecturing, and a lecturer is always recasting his work and using it in different forms. A lecturer has no prejudice against repetition. It is noticeable that in some of Emerson's important lectures the logical scheme is more perfect than in his essays. The truth seems to be that in the process of working up and perfecting his writings, in revising and filing his sentences, the logical scheme became more and more obliterated. Another circumstance helped make his style fragmentary. He was by nature a man of inspirations and exalted moods. He was subject to ecstasies, during which his mind worked with phenomenal brilliancy. Throughout his works and in his diary we find constant reference to these moods, and to his own inability to control or recover them. "But what we want is consecutiveness. 'T is with us a flash of light, then a long darkness, then a flash again. Ah! could we turn these fugitive sparkles into an astronomy of Copernican worlds!"

In order to take advantage of these periods of divination, he used to write down the thoughts that came to him at such times. From boyhood onward he kept journals and commonplace books, and in the course of his reading and meditation he collected innumerable notes and quotations which he indexed for ready use. In these mines he "quarried," as Mr. Cabot says, for his lectures and essays. When he needed a lecture he went to the repository, threw together what seemed to have a bearing on some subject, and gave it a title. If any other man should adopt this method of composition, the result would be incomprehensible chaos; because most men have many interests, many moods, many and conflicting ideas. But with Emerson it was otherwise. There was only one thought which could set him aflame, and that was the thought of the unfathomed might of man. This thought was his religion, his politics, his ethics, his philosophy. One moment of inspiration was in him own brother to the next moment of inspiration, although they might be separated by six weeks. When he came to put together his star-born ideas, they fitted well, no matter in what order he placed them, because they were all part of the same idea.

From "Emerson, Sixty Years After," *The Atlantic Monthly,* 79 (Jan. and Feb. 1897), 27-41 and 222-40.

THOMAS WENTWORTH HIGGINSON

MR. EMERSON'S fame extended far beyond his native land; and it is probable that no writer of the English tongue had more influence in England, thirty years ago, before the all-absorbing interest of the new theories of evolution threw all the so-called transcendental philosophy into temporary shade. When we consider, for instance, his marked influence on three men so utterly unlike one another as Carlyle, Tyndall, and Matthew Arnold, the truth of this remark can hardly be disputed. On the continent his most ardent admirers and commentators were Edgar Quinet in France, and Herman Grimm in Germany.

It will be remembered by many that during [Lajos] Kossuth's very remarkable tour in this country—when he adapted himself to the local traditions and records of every village as if he had just been editing for publication its local annals—he had the tact to identify Emerson, in his fine way, with Concord, and said in his speech there, turning to him, "You, sir, are a philosopher. Lend me, I pray you, the aid of your philosophical analysis," etc., etc. He addressed him, in short, as if he had been Kant or Hegel. But in reality nothing could be remoter from Emerson than such a philosophic type as this. He was only a philosopher in the vaguer ancient sense; his mission was to sit, like Socrates, beneath the plane-trees, and offer profound and beautiful aphorisms, without even the vague thread of the Socratic method to tie them together. Once, and once only, in his life, he seemed to be approaching the attitude of systematic statement—this being in his course of lectures on "The Natural Method of Intellectual Philosophy," given in 1868 or thereabouts; the fundamental proposition of these lectures being that "every law of nature is a law of mind," and all material laws are symbolical statements. These few lectures certainly inspired his admirers with the belief that their great poetic seer might commend himself to the systematizers also. But for some reason, even these lectures were not published till after Emerson's death, and his latest books had the same detached and fragmentary character as his earliest. He remained still among the poets, not among the philosophic doctors, and must be permanently classified in that manner.

Yet it may be fearlessly said that, within the limits of a single sentence, no man who ever wrote the English tongue has put more meaning into words than Emerson. In his hands, to adopt Ben Jonson's phrase, words "are rammed with thought." No one has reverenced the divine art of speech more than Emerson, or practiced it more nobly. "The Greeks," he once said in an unpublished lecture, "anticipated by their very language what the best orator could say;" and neither Greek precision nor Roman vigor could produce a phrase that Emerson could not match. Who stands in all literature as the master of condensation if not Tacitus? Yet Emerson, in his speech at the anti-Kansas meeting in Cambridge, quoted that celebrated remark by Tacitus when mentioning that the effigies of Brutus and Cassius were not carried at a certain State funeral; and in translating it, bettered the original. The indignant phrase of Tacitus is, "Praefulgebant . . . eo ipso quod . . . non visebantur," thus giving a grand moral lesson in six words; but Emerson gives it in five, and translates it, even more powerfully: "They glared through their absences." Look through all Emerson's writings, and then consider whether in all literature you can find a man who has better fulfilled that aspiration stated in such condensed words by Joubert, "to put a whole book into a page, a whole page into a phrase, and that phrase into a word." After all, it is phrases and words won like this which give immortality. And if you say that, nevertheless, this is nothing, so long as an author has not given us a system of the universe, it can only be said that Emerson never desired to do this, but left on record the opinion that "it is too young by some ages yet to form a creed." The system-makers have their place, no doubt; but when we consider how many of them have risen and fallen since Emerson began to write,— Coleridge, Schelling, Cousin, Comte, Mill, down to the Hegel of yesterday and the Spencer of to-day,—it is really evident that the absence of a system cannot prove much more short-lived than the possession of that commodity.

From "Ralph Waldo Emerson" in *Contemporaries* (Boston: Houghton, Mifflin, 1899), pp. 1-22.

Twentieth-Century Critical Essays

ROBERT LEE FRANCIS

The Architectonics of Emerson's *Nature*

AT FIRST GLANCE few essays could look so transparent. *Nature* begins with an "Introduction" and has a final chapter called, "Prospects." Between the beginning and end, there are seven chapters, respectively entitled: "Nature," "Commodity," "Beauty," "Language," "Discipline," "Idealism" and "Spirit." Yet on closer examination we discover that the chapters are of radically unequal length and that in terms of conventional logic we find it difficult to discover the transition from one chapter to the next. Beyond these problems we observe that one chapter, "Language," seems to command more attention than the others, undoubtedly because its organization and development seem more transparent and conventional than in the other chapters. Its very centrality in the essay and the nature of its definitions have led some critics to argue that the platonic aspect of the essay, underscored by the original motto of 1836, creates a division at this point between the first five chapters and the last four, that with this chapter we cross over the famous divided line of Plato from the world of impressions to the world of ideas. But there is a particular aspect of the chapter, "Language," which provides us with a clue to Emerson's strategy in the essay. For while the entire essay is an elaborate exercise in definition of the sort that the chapter, "Language," enumerates—that is, a movement from phenomenal experience to symbolic comprehension of noumenal experience in the phenomenal world—the specific gesture toward syllogistic formulation that is so conspicuously part of the chapter hints at a "scientific" approach. Part of the author's strategy in defining the "uses" of nature is to present himself not merely as spiritual philosopher but also as scientific naturalist.... The scientific naturalist begins by classifying and defining data, but he is ultimately engaged in ordering the human mind's conception of its own existence. To that end the naturalist becomes philosophic; he becomes poetic as well as systematic. This mode of defining is highly fluid, partaking of the interaction of matter and thought, of natural facts and spiritual facts....

If we examine the first two sections of the essay, we confront a series of definitions characterized by great fluidity. The "Introduction" contains four paragraphs. The first two constitute a general approach to the large topic of the essay. The first is interrogative and evocative; the second is declarative and imperative. The first begins with an assertion about the past and concludes with an injunction for the future. The second paragraph begins with a sweeping generalization and concludes with the crucial question of the essay. The third and fourth paragraphs are quite concrete. The third approaches the topic from the perspective of science; the fourth from the perspective of philosophy. The third poses a series of value judgments concerning the scientific approach to nature; the fourth undertakes a series of definitions of the central term and its subcategories. Thus the "Introduction" moves from a series of oratorical flourishes to some rhetorical distinctions and definitions. In contrast to this introduction, the first chapter of the essay makes a highly personal statement about how we perceive what has just been defined. The approach here is in contrast to the striving for objectivity at the end of the introduction. We sense a strong personal voice which is not that of a mere impersonal scientific naturalist or quite that of the universal Orphic Poet, for it expresses itself in a series of highly meta-phoric statements about the phenomenal world that culminates in that metaphor of vital spatial vision—the transparent eyeball (still maligned, even by Jonathan Bishop in his otherwise sensitive reading of Emerson on the Soul). The voice moves from the familiar and concrete (the speaker is scuddling through the winter puddles of a common) to a bizarrely vivid attempt at a universal symbol appropriate both to natural anatomy and spiritual insight which is the climax of the fourth paragraph. Then the "occult relation" between man and his world is treated subjectively in the fifth paragraph; and finally in the sixth para-graph that relationship is objectively crystallized in the epigram: "Nature always wears the color of the spirit." Thus in the first two sections of the essay, we encounter two kinds of definition. In the "Introduction" nature is defined as "essence unchanged by man" and art as "the mixture of man's will with those essences." These are essen-tially substantive definitions that operate near the "ground line of familiar facts." In contrast to these the final large observation of the first chapter, "Nature," does not operate as a substantive definition; it appears to be a highly poetic assertion that is epigrammatic but illusive. Yet, as Chapter VII, "Spirit," will reveal, such a mode of defining is as essential to Emerson as the more conventional way. Between these two modes of definition the remaining chapters of the essay modulate.

The next six chapters, as Emerson makes clear in the opening para-graph of Chapter II, partake of this essentially dialectical mode of development. Chapter II, "Commodity," deals with "those advantages which our senses owe to nature," in which Emerson sees nature not only as material substance but as process and result as well: "The wind sows the seed; the sun evaporates the sea; the wind blows the vapor to the field; the ice, the other side of the planet, condenses rain on this; the rain feeds the plant; the plant feeds the animal; and thus the endless circulations of the divine charity nourish man." The catalogue of such commodity and utility is, as Emerson notes, "endless." Chapter III, "Beauty," bears the same analogous relation to Chapter II that Chapter I bore to the "Introduction." Its opening line makes clear the more theoretical dimension of this section: "A nobler want of man is served by nature, namely the want of Beauty." A similar relationship is established between the chapter on "Language" and the chapter on "Discipline." The former is basically specific, like the section of definitions in the "Introduction" and like the concern with natural phenomena in "Commodity." On the other hand, "Discipline" defines a more theoretical concept and to that extent is more like "Beauty." This relationship of the specific to the theoretical also exists between the chapters on "Idealism" and "Spirit"; for idealism as an *ism* lends itself to specific definition and classification, whereas spirit must be intuitively and poetically apprehended.

In terms of its structure *Nature* moves through a series of chapters in which not only a relationship between the specific and the theoretical is established but each pair of chapters leads to an increasingly more complex set of concepts. For example, though "Language" might be said to be more complex in its definitional structure than the stipulative terms in the "Introduction," and while "Idealism" might be said to be even more complex than "Language" in the nature and scope of its definitions; yet each, in retrospective relation to what follows, seems relatively simple. What we experience is a definitional escalation. In this fashion Emerson is able to move from the minutiae which are principally the concern of the scientific naturalist to the metaphoric speculations which are the primary concern of the artist as Orphic Poet. From what we glean in Emerson's letters and journal entries, we can recognize his structural intentions in these terms. We know, for example, that when he decided to add to his "little book" the essay, "Spirit," on which he was working separately, he was troubled by the transition from "Discipline" to "Spirit." The chapter on "Idealism" which he then wrote, serves as a specific concrete bridge and completes the pattern of complementary chapters. In such a structural scheme, the final chapter, "Prospects," stands as a summation of the whole work. This sense of mounting dialectic definition is also supported by the motto of 1849, with its clear emphasis on the evolving, upward aspiration of the worm to be man. Indeed this later motto suggests that the chapters are not merely a series of ladder rungs but constitute demarcations on a helixical spire of form which the 1849 motto vividly describes. Accordingly we are invited both to pair the chapters and to see them in some sort of helixical evolutionary scheme, moving from very finite data to the larger realms of spirit and to the prospects beyond about which the Orphic Poet, the final voice of the author, sings so prophetically. . . .

This "double vision" is most evident in the more theoretical chapters of *Nature*: "Beauty," "Discipline" and "Spirit." In the chapter

"Beauty," for example, Emerson first tried to suggest the complex possibilities of beauty in a single paragraph; but he wisely recognized that such an approach was too abstract, too illusive. What the first paragraph tries to convey is the eye's response to several aspects of beauty simultaneously. But Emerson must intuitively have sensed that the reader might need to recognize the parts first before he could see the whole, and so he began the next paragraph: "For better consideration, we may distribute the aspects of Beauty in a threefold manner." As we analyze the three separate aspects, we see that they are delight, virtue and intellect. Returning then to the observation of the first paragraph, we see how the eye should see these three aspects of beauty simultaneously in cosmic harmony. Each represents a single dimension of the whole; but they are ordered in relation to their increasing complexity. That is, delight is essentially simple sensuous response; virtue is sensuous response combined with human will; and intellect is sensuous response related to thought that is itself related to human will. Consequently for Emerson "Beauty, in the largest and profoundest sense, is one expression for the universe. . . . Truth, goodness, and beauty are but different faces of the same All." In the final paragraph Emerson returns to where he began, weaving the three strands back together and leaving the reader with a more articulated sense of that first formulation, beyond which the chapter has not really gone. . . .

What is truly significant about *Nature* is what Emerson did with this rather conventional Romantic notion [of the artist emulating nature]. For what, as we now see in "Prospects," the Poet-Naturalist creates is not merely churches or paintings or poems but no less than Man himself. The Poet-Naturalist becomes the architect of man. We should have guessed this fact from the beginning; for quite early, in "Commodity," Emerson quoted two lines from George Herbert's poem, "Man." Here, in "Prospects," he quotes five stanzas. The first line is prophetic of the whole Emersonian perspective: "Man is all symmetry." The ending to the essay, which is no conclusion in the conventional rhetorical sense, is simply but grandly the recognition of symmetry, the shaping of the capstone to the broken arch. *Nature* is, then, a blueprint, an architectonic, for the construction of the self out of the world's body, of the *me* out of the *not me*. This imaginative act of creation is an affirmation of the transcendent truth of man's divine nature.

From "The Architectonics of Emerson's *Nature*," *American Quarterly*, 19 (Spring 1967), 39-52.

KENNETH BURKE

I, Eye, Ay—Emerson's Early Essay on "Nature"

SINCE BOTH tragic catharsis and dialectical transcendence involve *formal development*, by the same token both modes give us kinds of *transformation*.

In tragic catharsis (or, more generally, dramatic catharsis—for there are corresponding processes in comedy), the principle of transformation comes to a focus in *victimage* The tragic pleasure requires a *symbolic sacrifice*—or, if you will, a *goat*. And the same is obviously true of the comic pleasure.

In dialectical transcendence, the principle of transformation operates in terms of a "beyond". It is like . . . the "priestly" function, in that it pontificates, or "builds a bridge" between disparate realms. And insofar as things here and now are treated in terms of a "beyond", they thereby become infused or inspirited by the addition of a *new* or *further dimension*.

The Emerson essay is a delightful example of such a terministic process. . . .

Essentially, the dialectical operations in the Emerson essay are to be built around the traditional One-Many (unity-diversity) pair. Emerson states it succinctly: "ascent from particular to general"; for if we say "furniture" instead of "tables, chairs, and carpets", we spontaneously speak of the more general term as in some way "higher". The process is completed when one has arrived at "highly" generalized terms like "entities" or "beings"—whereupon all that is left is a further step to something like "Pure Being", or the One, or First, or Ultimate, or some such. When we arrive at this stage, the over-all term-of-terms or title-of-titles is so comprehensive it is simultaneously nowhere and everywhere. Hence, mystics can select just about anything, no matter how lowly and tangible, to stand for it (for instance, the enigmatic role of the wasp, as seen by Mrs. Moore and imagined by Professor Godbole in *A Passage to India*). Dialectical transcendence depends upon these quite pedestrian resources of terminology.

In the case of Emerson's essay, the underlying structure is as simple as this: The everyday world, all about us here and now, is to be interpreted as a *diversity* of *means* for carrying out a *unitary purpose* (or, if you will, the *principle* of purpose) that is situated in an ultimate realm *beyond* the here and now. The world's variety of things is thus to be interpreted *in terms of* a transcendent unifier (that infuses them all with its single spirit). And by this mode of interpretation all the world comes to be viewed as a set of *instrumentalities*. (Emerson more resonantly calls them "commodities".) For we should bear it in mind that Emerson's brand of transcendentalism was but a short step ahead of out-and-out pragmatism. . . .

Here is what I take to be the underlying form of the essay:

It treats of Society in terms of Nature—and it treats of Nature in terms of the Supernatural. Thereby even the discussion of Society in its most realistic aspects becomes transcendentally tinged (somewhat as though you had made a quite literal line drawing with pen and ink, and had covered it with a diaphanous wash of cerulean blue).

In keeping with such an approach to the everyday materials of living, note how even the realm of the sensory can be interpreted as a kind of *revelation*. For whatever the world is, in its sheer brute nature as physical vibrations or motions it *reveals itself* to us *in terms* of sights, sounds, tastes, scents, touch, summed up as pleasure or pain. Thus you already have the terministic conditions whereby even the most material of sensations can be called "apocalyptic" (since the word but means "revealing")—and Emerson does apply precisely that word. In this respect, even the crudest of sensory perceptions can be treated as the revealing of nature's mysteries, though the revelations are confined to the restrictions imposed upon us by the physical senses that reveal them. Also, the resources of dialectic readily permit us to make a further step, insofar as particulars can be treated in terms that transcend their particularity. Within the Emersonian style, this convenience indigenous to terminology would be more resonantly stated: "when the fact is seen in the light of an idea".

If Nature is to be treated in terms of Supernature, another possibility presents itself. There could be stylistic procedures designed to serve as *bridges* (or intermediaries) between the two sets of terms. The simplest instance of such a bridging device is to be seen in the dialectic of Christian theology. If you make a distinction between "God" and "Man", you set up the terministic conditions for an intermediate term (for bridging the gap between the two orders): namely, "God-man". Similarly, in the dialectic of psychoanalysis, one might be advised to inquire whether the term "pre-conscious" can serve (at least on some occasions) as a bridge between the terms "conscious" and "unconscious". Fittingly, the major bridge of this sort in Emerson's essay comes in the chapter halfway through, containing the homily on "Discipline". . . .

The chapter on "Discipline" serves as a bridge between the *Hic et Nunc* and the "Beyond". To appreciate the dialectical maneuvers here, we should lay great stress upon the strategic sentence in the Introduction: "Let us inquire, to what end is nature?" This question sets the conditions for the pattern of development. Of all the issues that keep recurring in the maneuvers of dialectic, surely none is more frequent than the theme of the One and the Many. As I have said, I feel that it is grounded in the logological fact that terms for particulars can be classified under some titular head. And thus, when we say "the Universe", we feel that we really are talking about the Universe, about "everything", though the term certainly includes an awful lot that we don't know anything about. (And I leave it for you to decide whether you can talk about something when you don't know what it is that you may be talking about.)

Be that as it may, given the typical resources of terminology, the question "To what end is nature?" allows for a one-many alignment of this sort: The world of our empirical existence can be viewed not just as a great variety of *things*, but as a great variety of *means*, all related to some ultimate *end*. In this regard we can see how Emerson's dialectic pattern (of *manifold means* in the world of everyday experience emblematically or hieroglyphically announcing some *unitary end* in a realm beyond everyday experience) set up the conditions for transcendentalizing maneuvers that would be progressively transformed into William James's pragmatism and John Dewey's instrumentalism. Though work, in its *utilitarian* aspects, amasses *material* powers, in its *ethical* aspects work can be felt to *transcend* utility. Hence "Discipline" serves as the means of crossing from sheer expediency to edification.

Before the bridge, Emerson's stress is upon *uses* (a subject dear to his countrymen, who were to build, by their technology, the highest Babylonian tower of useful things the world has ever known, though many of the uses were to prove worse than useless). In his case, of course, the many resources of utility are moralized in terms of a transcendental purpose, itself in the realm *beyond* the bridge. On this side the bridge, there are "Commodity", "Beauty", and "Language". "Beauty" endangers the design, inasmuch as it is an end in itself. But Emerson preserves the design by his concluding decision that "beauty in nature is not ultimate". It is "the herald of inward and eternal beauty".

Nothing could more quickly reveal the terministic resources of the Emersonian dialectic (or, if you will, the Emersonian unction) than contrasting his views on language with Jeremy Bentham's "theory of fictions". Bentham laid major stress upon the fact that all our terms for spiritual or psychological states are initially terms for sheerly physical things and processes. And by "fictions" he had in mind the thought that all moral or psychological nomenclatures are essentially metaphors carried over from the physical realm and applied analogically. But Emerson's transcendental dialectic allows him to apply a tender-minded mode of interpretation, thus:

> Words are signs of natural facts. The use of natural history is to give us aid in supernatural history; the use of the outer creation, to give us language for the beings and changes of the inward creation. Every word which is used to express a moral or intellectual fact, if

traced to its root, is found to be borrowed from some material appearance. *Right* means *straight*; *wrong* means *twisted*. *Spirit* primarily means *wind*; *transgression*, the crossing of a *line*; *supercilious*, the *raising of the eyebrow*. We say the *heart* to express emotion, the *head* to denote thought; and *thought* and *emotion* are words borrowed from sensible things, and now appropriated to spiritual nature.

And so on. In any case, once you thus turn things around, you see why, if the things of nature are to serve us by providing us with terms which we can apply analogically for the development of a moral terminology, the whole subject then would come to a focus in a chapter on nature itself as a source of moral "discipline". Fittingly, the chapter begins by reference to the *"use of the world"* as a discipline. And at the beginning of the next chapter, "Idealism", we read: "To this one *end* of Discipline, all parts of nature conspire." (Italics in both cases mine.) Thus, when the chapter on "Discipline" is over, we have gone from the realm of *means* to the realm of *ends* or, more specifically, one unitary end (or, if you will, the sheer *principle* of purpose).

Fittingly, now that we have crossed the bridge, into the realm of "Reason" and "Spirit", Nature suffers what Emerson himself calls a "degrading". For whereas Nature rated high when thought of as leading towards the Supernatural, in comparison with the Supernatural it comes into question, even as regards its material existence. (Incidentally, this change of rating in Emerson's dialectic corresponds, in the Marxian dialectic, to a step such as the transformation of the bourgeoisie from the class that is the bearer of the future to the class that is to be buried by the future. In a ladder of developments, rung 5 is "progressive" with regard to rung 3, but "reactionary" with regard to rung 7.) However, in this later "degrading" of nature, he pauses to admonish: "I do not wish to fling stones at my beautiful mother, nor soil my gentle nest." He wishes, in effect, but to complete the tracking down of the positions implicit in his dialectic.

One final development should be mentioned, since it throws a quite relevant light upon the essay's methods. In his final chapter, "Prospects", while zestfully reciting the many steps that man has taken through the course of history towards the affirming of what Emerson takes to be the ultimate supernatural Oneness, the essay has so built up the promissory that we scarcely note how airily the problem of evil is dismissed:

Build therefore your own world. As fast as you conform your life to the pure idea in your mind, that will unfold its great proportions. A correspondent revolution in things will attend the influx of the spirit. So fast will disagreeable appearances, swine, spiders, snakes, pests, mad-houses, prisons, enemies, vanish; they are temporary and shall be no more seen. [This comes close to the line in "Lycidas": "Shall now no more be seen".] The sordor and filths of nature, the sun shall dry up and the wind exhale. As when the summer comes from the south the snow-banks melt and the face of the earth becomes green before it, so shall the advancing spirit create its ornaments along its path, and carry with it the beauty it visits and the song which enchants it. . . .

He envisions in sum "the kingdom of man over nature".

One can't do anything with that, other than to note that it disposes of many troublesome things in a great hurry. But the Marxist dialectic is not without an analogous solution, in looking upon the socialist future as "inevitable". . . .

As regards "the thinking of the body", there are strong hints of a fecal motive near the end of the section on "Language":

'Material objects,' said a French philosopher, 'are necessarily kinds of *scoriae* of the substantial thoughts of the Creator, which must always preserve an exact relation to their first origin; in other words, visible nature must have a spiritual and moral side.'

I have found that readers seldom look up the word *scoriae*. It comes from the same root as "scatological". Here it conceives the realm of matter as nothing other than God's *offal*. Such images are likely to turn up somewhere in the dialectics of transformation, especially where there is talk of "discipline". . . .

At the end of the chapter on "Discipline", just before we cross to the realm of the Beyond, we find traces of victimage, in his solemnizing references to separation from a friend:

When much intercourse with a friend has supplied us with a standard of excellence, and has increased our respect for the resources of God who thus sends a real person to outgo our ideal; when he has, moreover, become an object of thought, and, whilst his character retains all its unconscious effect, is converted in the mind into solid and sweet wisdom,—it is a sign to us that his office is closing, and he is commonly withdrawn from our sight in a short time.

Is not this passage a euphemism for the death, or near-death, of a close friend? And thus, does not the bridge that carries us across to the Beyond end on strong traces of tragic dignification by victimage?

From "I, Eye, Ay—Emerson's Early Essay on 'Nature': Thoughts on the Machinery of Transcendence," *The Sewanee Review*, 74 (Autumn 1966), 875-95.

JOEL PORTE

Nature as Symbol: Emerson's Noble Doubt

EMERSON WAS driven to accept the Ideal theory because he found sense experience distasteful, but not at all because he really believed that the world was an illusion. Convinced by temperament and training that the mind and the body, the spirit and nature, were not only separate but unequal, that the soul was higher, finer, truer than matter, he need a theory, other than Christianity, that would bestow intellectual dignity upon these sentiments. Idealism was the answer. It would serve the double purpose of presenting Emerson as a humble, self-abnegating prophet of the one true religion, while at the same time implying his aristocratic nature. Through applying the Ideal theory to nature, he could justify his fastidious tastes on the grounds of a seemingly Romantic philosophy, and perhaps even prove ultimately that he was a better citizen than most people thought. But an avowal of idealism also had its dangers: the taint of otherworldliness, with its damning implications of "orientalism" and "moonshine"; the horrors of scepticism (as Emerson once put it, the "slow suicide" of a Schopenhauer); and, finally, the possibility of hypocrisy—a besetting sin of the Protestant world-view since Puritan times. . . .

For Emerson, idealism was meant to strengthen the backbone of nineteenth-century youths by turning them from pleasure to pious performance: the lotus, either as a food or as a position, was not being recommended. . . .

[Richard] Price avoided the possible problem of the dualism of mind and matter inherent in idealism by resolutely ignoring the puzzles of epistemology. The promptings of spirit and the promptings of matter are equally real, but spirit is better. Emerson ultimately ended up in the same position, but he did—perhaps unfortunately— broach the epistemological problem in his desire to win converts from matter to spirit. In the end, of course, he attempted to resolve the problem, but simply by a strategy of self-reliance, and not in any philosophically rigorous fashion.

Emerson, like Price, clearly had no use for scepticism, especially when it was of the railing kind: "The frivolous make themselves merry with the Ideal theory, as if its consequences were burlesque; as if it affected the stability of nature. It surely does not." Yet Emerson's idealism, on its ontological side, certainly did seem to affect the stabil-

ity of matter, as it questioned the reliability of perception on its epistemological side. Emerson himself never tired of saying that matter is
accidental, and this would naturally tend to cast doubt on its stability.
But, in fact, Emerson never really meant to question the stability of
nature: it was its intrinsic value he doubted. In his zeal, however, to
"put nature underfoot," he unfortunately seemed to will it out of
existence. Emerson did this by resolving the problem of epistemological
dualism much to the disadvantage of nature. Faced with the disparity
between perception and the thing perceived, Emerson decided that the
instability lay in nature rather than in the mind of the beholder.
Clearly, if the world of perception is the "true" one, then the so-called
"real" world is phenomenal, a shifting dream which cannot be trusted.
Having established that the perception is the supreme arbiter of reality
—that the mind is the true guide to knowledge—Emerson used this
argument to resolve the problem of psychophysical dualism in favor of
"mental" entities. That is, "ideas," such as Truth, Goodness, and Justice, he considered to be the only real existents, having their home in
the mind of the noble doubter; "things" he considered to be mere
appearances, shadows and symbols perhaps of divine truth, but worth-
less in themselves.

Once he had established that the intuitions of a noble soul have
precedence, as truth, over sense experience, Emerson was quite willing
to allow the world to go on existing. His aim had been to resolve,
without Christianity, the Christian dualism between flesh and spirit in
favor of spirit, and to this end he happily pre-empted the arguments of
a sceptical solipsist. But he balked at the dangerous conclusions of the
latter: "Yet, if it [idealism] only deny the existence of matter, it does
not satisfy the demands of the spirit. It leaves God out of me. It leaves
me in the splendid labyrinth of my perceptions, to wander without
end." We should note that, for Emerson, scepticism is bad not because
it leaves God out of the universe, but because it leaves God out of man:
it denies self-reliance (which, for Emerson, is God-reliance, since God—
the moral law—resides in man). But Emerson had solved the problem
before stating it by simply asserting, in the manner of an arrogant
Descartes, the epistemological and ontological stability of man's spirit:
I think truth, therefore I am true. So that idealism, for Emerson, ends
up "merely as a useful introductory hypothesis, serving to apprize us of
the eternal distinction between the soul and the world." The noble
doubt should serve to inspire self-reverence and a belief in "ideas," and
not universal uncertainty. . . .

Emerson, in fact, thought he knew perfectly well what nature
meant, and devoted his *Nature* to an assertion of that meaning. Indeed,
Emerson's own sad admission that there was a "crack" in his first book
between the chapters on "Discipline" and "Idealism" may appear to be
overly harsh self-criticism to a reader who has come to terms with what

Emerson's idealism really signifies—a simple denial of the inherent worth of matter and sense experience. All of *Nature* has one theme, and there is actually no disparity between and among its sections. In the chapter on "Commodity," for instance, we learn that "a man is fed, not that he may be fed, but that he may work." Nature serves to enable man to do his duty, and not to allow him to rest slothfully in his pleasure. Nor does the section on "Beauty" contradict this stern dictum, although Emerson seems to suggest that aesthetic satisfaction is an end in itself when he states that "the world . . . exists to the soul to satisfy the desire of beauty. This element I call an ultimate end." He quickly adds the warning that "beauty in nature is not ultimate." Virtue, we realize, is what beauty really exists to imply. In the next section we find that language serves as the medium of expression for parables of moral truth, and that nature functions as the symbol of spirit, when spirit equals the human mind and the latter implies ethical awareness. This reading is made explicit in the chapter on "Discipline." Emerson tells us that "sensible objects conform to the premonitions of Reason and reflect the conscience." Things "hint or thunder to man the laws of right and wrong, and echo the Ten Commandments," and "the moral law lies at the centre of nature. . . ."

It is then no great feat to realize that *Nature* ends by being a hymn to progress under the moral law. It predicts the "kingdom of man over nature," rather than the perfection of man in himself through a renewed contact with the physical world.

From "Nature as Symbol: Emerson's Noble Doubt," *The New England Quarterly,* 37 (Dec. 1964), 453-76.

HENRY NASH SMITH

Emerson's Problem of Vocation:
A Note on "The American Scholar"

ONE OF the earliest phases of Emerson's concern with [his own] vocation may be observed in the notion of 'character' which appears in [Emerson's] *Journals* in 1828. Character stands at first for a confident acquiescence in God's perfect governance of the universe. From another point of view character is interpreted as global integrity, self-sufficiency, self-reliance resulting from the soul's "absolute command of its desires," with a corresponding loss of solicitude concerning what other men do. The idea lends itself, again, to a Neoplatonic declaration of the unreality of all action, concerned as it necessarily is with the realm of mere phenomena and of evil. Yet character can also become— very significantly—the equivalent of lawless, irrational genius, a synonym of the German's "*Daimonisches*"; and so desperate is Emerson's concern to defend his ideal of passivity against "carpenters, masons, and merchants" who "pounce on him" for his supposed idleness that he can resort to an almost physiological determinism, maintaining that God "has given to each his calling in his ruling love, . . . has adapted the brain and the body of men to the work that is to be done in the world." If some men "have a contemplative turn, and voluntarily seek solitude and converse with themselves," in God's name, he exclaims with surprising heat, let them alone!

The famous address on "The American Scholar" is in large part but a summary of these and other ideas that had been recurring in the *Journals* for a decade. Character is recognized here as the special attribute of the Contemplative Man; and it is noteworthy that the address contains a long and confused discussion of the issue of Action *versus* Contemplation. Emerson is still troubled by the popular conception of the Scholar as a recluse, realizing that such an interpretation makes contemplative inaction a species of valetudinarianism; and he seeks to redeem the Scholar from the implied charge of weakness and cowardice. Yet the passage on the value of manual labor in enriching a writer's vocabulary merely confuses the issue by using "action" in a new sense; and the praise of action because it is "pearls and rubies to [the Scholar's] discourse" seems almost *fin de siècle* in its subordination of life to art. Only by an extreme irony or a thoroughly artistic failure to distinguish the actual from the imagined can Emerson go on to exclaim, "I run eagerly into this resounding tumult [of the world]. I grasp the hands of those next me, and take my place in the ring to suffer and to work. . . ." And the proposed end is still merely literary: the Scholar enters the world not in order to reform it, but in order that the dumb abyss of his inarticulate thought may become "vocal with speech." A deeper level of Emerson's meaning appears in the warning that the Scholar, in committing himself to action (here in its usual sense of humanitarian reform), runs the danger of forfeiting his self-reliance to the tyranny of "the popular judgments and modes of action." And at the end of the address the Contemplative Man's scrutiny is directed to "the perspective of [his] own infinite life"—that is, integrity, character —to be explored and developed by introspection. It hardly settles the issue to add to the Scholar's "study and . . . communication of principles" the further task of "making those instincts prevalent, the conversion of the world." For the original problem was the choice of a means —active reform or passive meditation—for converting the world. Emerson's refusal to choose between these alternatives is highly significant. On the one hand it reveals again the essentially contemplative nature of his Scholar-ideal; on the other it shows his curious reluctance to surrender the Scholar's claim to the contradictory virtues of the active reformer.

It has become customary to interpret "The American Scholar" as a statement of literary nationalism. But in the light of Emerson's prolonged struggle with the problem of vocation, the nationalistic phase of the address seems of diminished importance. Emerson was struggling to affirm a creed of self-reliance, and the fiction of the Scholar was a phase of the struggle. To the extent that the intellectual domination of Europe interferes with the Scholar's integrity, he must of course throw it off. But Europe is by no means the Scholar's worst enemy. His hardest struggles are civil and American: with vulgar prosperity; with the tyranny of the past; with "the popular cry," even though this be momentarily for some good thing—in short, with all the forces against which Emerson was striving to protect the inarticulate secrets of his own mind, the intuitive belief in his personal mission.

Impressive as the fiction of the Scholar was for Emerson's contemporaries, it did not bring about at this time a permanent equilibrium of conflicting impulses within the author himself. The address contains no coherent statement of the Scholar's positive functions. In many respects Emerson's situation in 1837 was the same as it had been five years before, when he withdrew from the pulpit; he had made concrete discoveries concerning what he must deny, but had not found a tangible alternative to the program of the reformers. He was still disturbed by his inability to renounce the ethical ideal of overt action.

From "Emerson's Problem of Vocation: A Note on 'The American Scholar,' " *The New England Quarterly*, 12 (March 1939), 52-67.

GEORGE EDWARD WOODBERRY

Emerson's "Divinity School Address"

THE SECOND notable occasion [the first was the Phi Beta Kappa Address] on which Emerson put forth a practical application of his thought was the delivery of the Divinity School Address, also at Harvard, July 15, 1838. In this he engaged himself more closely with the times and dealt in particular with the state of religion in the community. He dwelt on the decay of religion in the churches and sought for the source and remedy of this condition. He attacked historical Christianity, of which the church of tradition is the institution, and he concentrated his criticism upon the sacred authority that belongs to the person of Christ as the divine that became human and thenceforth the lawgiver of the soul in the Christian world. The course of the argument is plain . . . The authority of the church had already been abolished [in Emerson's view] by the doctrine of the self-sufficiency of the soul by virtue of its intuitive faculty which is the sole means of truth. With regard to Christ, Emerson reversed the old conception; instead of a divine person becoming human, he is a human person becoming divine, and the chief illustration of that process of perfection by which every soul unites with the divine; but he differs from others only in the degree of his progress, nor does his superiority vest him with authority over others, any more than in the case of Goethe, but each soul must follow the path of and from himself and draw strength, not from Christ, but from that common source which, as it once fed the soul of Christ, now feeds every soul born into the world of Nature. The doctrine of the equality of souls is applied to Christ as to all other masters of the past. Emerson also indicated, though less clearly, a fresh position or corollary. "The soul," he said, "knows no persons." This denied the personality of God; nor did he at any time figure deity as a form of personal being. The general plea, urged with great spirituality of feeling, was that men should abandon the past, that is, in this case, the church and Christ as its head, and no longer seek truth there, but should return to the living fountain of the divine in themselves.

The Address stirred the waters of controversy. The authorities of the Divinity School felt it necessary to disown the opinions set forth. Dr. Ware, the friend and predecessor of Emerson in the Old North Church, preached a kindly sermon, defining the serious nature of the bearing of these ideas in subverting Christianity, and Dr. Andrews Norton denounced them as an irruption of German atheism in the community. There were many pamphlets, discourses, and criticisms. Emerson stood aloof from all, seemingly indifferent though annoyed by the publicity that the agitation caused. Dr. Ware, however, drew from him a remarkably plain statement of his intellectual method and the ground of his conviction in general. He wrote, in reply to a friendly letter, excusing himself from any polemical statement: "I could not give account of myself if challenged. I could not possibly give you one of the 'arguments' you cruelly hint at, on which any doctrine of mine stands; for I do not know what arguments mean in reference to any expression of a thought. I delight in telling what I think; but if you ask me how I dare say so, or why it is so, I am the most helpless of mortal men." The claim of intuition to immediate knowledge could not be more lucidly presented than in this declaration.

Emerson loved the church. He never ceased to be at heart a minister; he was preaching at this time in Unitarian pulpits, and he continued to preach, though with diminishing frequency, for nine years after this Address. He seems never to have understood why his doctrines could not be consistently put forth at the Christian assembly on the Sabbath, for he regarded the Sabbath and the office of preaching as the greatest benefits that Christianity had transmitted to the social life. He valued traditional religion in a threefold way. He retained the sentiment for the old-time Sabbath day and often refers to its disappearance with regret, both for its atmosphere of external quiet and for its devotional joy in the gathered congregations in the meeting-houses. He retained also a deeply founded respect for the old-fashioned Calvinism of his ancestry, as a form of strong character and fervid piety. "What a debt is ours to that old religion," he exclaims, "which in the childhood of most of us still dwelt like a Sabbath morning in the country of New England, teaching privation, self-denial, and sorrow. A man was born not for prosperity, but to suffer for the benefit of others, like the noble rock-maple which all around our villages bleeds for the service of man. Not praise, not men's acceptance of our doing, but the spirit's holy errand through us absorbed the thought. How dignified was this!" It is a sincere motion of patriotism, of faith to the country of our origins, that beats in this passage—the voice of an old dweller on the soil; and this respect, that is half sad affection, Emerson was rich in. Lastly, he valued traditional religion in a less attractive way, as a concession to a lower type of intelligence and culture, as the best of which its adherents were capable of receiving, and as, at its lowest, a useful police power. There was this much of accommodation in his mind. He had made Carlyle's discovery of "the fool-part of man," and ten years before this time he had applied it to the interpretations of Scripture given by the New Jerusalem Church. "The interpretation is doubtless wholly false," he says, "and if the fool-part of man must have the lie, if truth is a pill that can't go down till it is sugared with superstition,—why, then I will forgive the last, in the belief that truth will enter into the soul so natively and assimilantly that it will become part of the soul, and so remain when the falsehood becomes dry and peels off." A similar view remained in his mind with regard to all forms of religious teaching, and harmonized with that invincible predisposition to value ideas for their moral energy rather than their intellectual purity, for their effect on life rather than their mental precision. In this spirit, and from a position conscious of superiority, he saw traditional religion continue in another level of life with content and even satisfaction. But whenever he spoke, despite his attachments to the old faith in these various ways, he advanced an attack, however disguised in many forms, upon the establishment of Christianity; he sapped its bases in the mind, and on all occasions, whatever his topic, preached the divine authority of the soul itself in all life, free of every form of priest or creed or ritual, of church or Saviour, or of any God other than the inflowing divine essence whose operation is impersonal, private, and unshared with any other. Orthodoxy was a strong power in New England and comprised the mass of the people; his own sect of Unitarianism excluded him from their ranks, with the exception of a small group of radicals and their associates; it is not strange that, in such circumstances, Emerson, after the delivery of this Address, was commonly regarded as atheistical, anti-Christian, and dangerous. Condemnation was the more unqualified because attention was naturally given at first rather to what he denied than to what he affirmed; what he denied, all men understood; but what he affirmed, few, if any, clearly made out.

From *Ralph Waldo Emerson* (New York: Macmillan, 1907), pp.55-59.

STUART C. WOODRUFF

Emerson's "Self-Reliance" and "Experience": A Comparison

WHEN . . . we juxtapose "Self-Reliance" with a later essay like "Experience," we get a much more accurate and instructive impression of Emerson's ideas and of the frequent adjustments they underwent. As Emerson himself wrote in the latter essay—and "Self-Reliance" must have been one thing he had in mind—"I am not the novice I was fourteen, nor yet seven years ago." What he had learned since his novitiate was that "I should not ask for a rash effect from meditations, counsels, and the hiving of truths" and that "there is no power of expansion in men." How different from "Self-Reliance" in which Emerson tells us that for "the self-helping man" "all doors are flung wide" or that one must act so as to render "all circumstances indifferent." Although it would be inaccurate to assert that Emerson retreats steadily from an early untenable position, the shift in emphasis from *Essays, First Series* to *Essays, Second Series,* is too well established to be ignored.

Reading "Self-Reliance," we sense the early Emerson's impatience that the millenium is not at hand, the implicit conviction that were man but to break the mortal coils of "consistency" and "conformity," his apotheosis would be immediate and divinity would radiate unimpeded from the center. The key that Emerson has discovered is absolute faith in one's intuitive moral sense and he seems rather frustrated that no one will try the lock. One is almost persuaded to do so by the effective massing of aphorisms: "Trust thyself: every heart vibrates to that iron string;" "No law can be sacred to me but that of my own nature;" "A foolish consistency is the hobgoblin of little minds;" "Whoso would be a man, must be a nonconformist." It is almost as if Emerson were trying to exorcise the evil spirits of custom and fear by the sheer force of language alone, to beat down "emphatic trifles" with a well-turned phrase. The result is an essay which, at its best, is rhetorical legerdemain; at its worst a kind of cavalier bravado.

For example, Emerson's attitude toward philanthropy, so reminiscent of Thoreau's, is hardly put gracefully: "Are they *my* poor?" Nor can we accept as valid such a pronouncement as this: "Friend, client, child, sickness, fear, want, charity, all knock at once at thy closet door and say—'Come out unto us.' But keep thy state; come not into their confusion." What Emerson would have every man do is to imitate "the ever-blessed One," since "self-existence is the attribute of the Supreme

Cause." Man realizes the potential divinity within him to the extent that he acts in accord with it; "self-existence," that is, must also be man's principal "attribute" and aim. Of course, the real subject of "Self-Reliance" is not so much self-trust as the reward of self-trust which is Power. "Power," says Emerson, "is, in nature, the essential measure of right. Nature suffers nothing to remain in her kingdoms which cannot help itself." It is precisely this sense of power, so heady but deceptive, that accounts for the irritating effect "Self-Reliance" creates the more closely its message is studied. What is particularly annoying is Emerson's facile assumption that, but for "emphatic trifles," man could duplicate the attributes of the "Supreme Cause" and thus give moral choice the force of natural law.

The paradoxical truth is that Emerson's early vision is in a sense antidemocratic; the distance between the man who realizes his divine essence ("God is here within") and the man who cannot—or does not—is enormous. Even the Poet is unable to close the gap. Once granted the "Power," a man leaves the world of mundane affairs, with its myriad involvements and claims on his energies, and dwells amidst "things unseen." Even if it were obtainable, such virtuous power creates nothing more effective than an Olympian detachment serving only self. Society, which in "Self-Reliance" seems to be the aggregate of non-transcendentalists, is defined as "a conspiracy against the manhood of its members." Emerson's insistence upon the "infinitude of the private man" necessitates a corresponding disparagement of men en masse. Hence we find him arguing that "when the ignorant and the poor are aroused, when the unintelligent brute force that lies at the bottom of society is made to growl and mow, it needs the habit of magnanimity and religion to treat it godlike as a trifle of no concernment." Like patriotism, society becomes the last refuge of a scoundrel, or at least of a coward willing to barter self-reliance for the sake of consistency and conformity.

Just what brought Emerson back to earth in the years separating "Self-Reliance" and "Experience" need not be dealt with here; by means of comparison the essays make their own case in their own terms. Read vis-a-vis, these essays reveal a movement from the world as it should be to the world as it is, from a euphoric mood of limitless expansion and potential to one of gnawing uncertainty and limitation, from impatience to a plea for "patience, patience." At every point the language itself of "Experience" suggests the change; one is struck forcibly by such phrases as these, absent in "Self-Reliance": "retreating," "degrade," "deluges of lethe," "routine," "contracts," "opium," "gross sense." The images of sleep and lethean stupor with which the essay opens suggest Emerson's frustration over the difficulties involved in achieving his earlier God-man ideal. Why, he wonders, was nature "so sparing of her fire and so liberal of her earth?" Like all romantics,

Emerson is now caught on the backswing of his emotional pendulum—from a deeply felt awareness of the ideal state of man to an equally keen sense of the obstacles that thwart its achievement. These obstacles are the very same "emphatic trifles" he brushed aside in "Self-Reliance." In "Experience," he refers to them by such oblique names as "Illusion, Temperament, Succession, Surface." They are now the "lords of life" and their effect is to rob man of his rightful heritage of power —to make of him a diminished thing. "Very mortifying," writes Emerson, "is the reluctant experience that some unfriendly excess or imbecility neutralizes the promise of genius." Here is compensation with a vengeance!

In "Self-Reliance," Emerson refers to self-trust as "that iron string." Curiously, in "Experience" he uses the same image, but with a far different meaning, when he speaks of "Temperament" as "that iron wire on which the beads ["train of moods"] are strung." What Emerson is dealing with here is the problem of subjective reality, both its nature and its reliability as the test of truth. Moods—the promptings of the senses and of the understanding—dominate us. Whereas in "Self-Reliance" Emerson challenges man to master circumstances, in "Experience" he sees man as the frequent victim of circumstances, both external and inherent in his very nature. "What cheer can the religious sentiment yield," Emerson asks, "when that is suspected to be secretly dependent on the seasons of the year and the state of the blood?" If we recall that in "Self-Reliance" Emerson claims that his perception of the "primary wisdom" of "Intuition" was "as much a fact as the sun," we get a good idea of the tension in his thinking. Although he extricates himself from the dilemma of temperament by assigning it to a lower order of reality, final only upon its own terms, he acknowledges its force.

Emerson's early concern with moral power alone becomes modified in "Experience" by the inclusion of form and the explicit acknowledgement of duality in both man and the universe. If intuition is the test of things unseen, experience is the equally valid test of things seen. Both, Emerson now realizes, have their due. In fact, Emerson asserts that life will be "sweet and sound" only if power and form are properly comingled. The tone of regret that underlies "Experience" stems from Emerson's sober awareness that man's innate divinity cannot be made manifest merely by willing it. With this awareness come a sympathy and a humility lacking in the earlier essays. Now the "universal impulse to believe" becomes more important than the nature of the belief itself. In "Experience" Emerson is keenly aware of the transitoriness of man's sense of innate divinity: "Like a bird which alights nowhere, but hops perpetually from bough to bough, is the Power which abides in no man and in no woman." Because these moments are so elusive, they must be husbanded. From an earlier position of urging man to tap the limitless power within him, Emerson comes almost full circle in "Experience" in his concept of conservation and prudence. Having returned somewhat singed from his earlier flights into the empyrean, Emerson can now assert "the mid-world is best." It is the mood of "the temperate zone" that helps to define the principal difference between the two essays and the balanced vision Emerson eventually achieved.

What makes "Experience" so much more interesting and trenchant than "Self-Reliance" is the fact that although Emerson hangs on doggedly to his general idea of man's divine nature, reaffirming its final triumph, he faces honestly those forces which limit and even contradict the "infinitude" of the private man. "The line he must walk," Emerson writes in "Experience," "is a hair's breadth." Below lies the "nightmare" of a chaotic amoral universe. It is to Emerson's credit as thinker that he balances so successfully; the very difficulty of such a feat stirs our sympathy and our admiration. Curiously, man's stature grows as it shrinks, in "Experience," in the face of a frequently inscrutable and whimsical universe; that is, he becomes ennobled by facing up to the magnitude of the forces which oppose him and the living of his dream. In calling man "a golden impossibility," Emerson comes finally to a wise understanding of the paradox, if not the tragedy, of the "human situation."

From "Emerson's 'Self-Reliance' and 'Experience': A Comparison," *The Emerson Society Quarterly*, No. 47 (1967), pp. 48-50.

ROBERT DETWEILER

The Over-Rated "Over-Soul"

AN OFTEN unavoidable part of the critical process, in the necessary dependence upon previous research, is the perpetration of errors along with the exposition of truth. Some of the errors become classic; a minor one may be the persistent use of *Over-Soul* as a central concept in Ralph Waldo Emerson's philosophy. It comes as something of a shock to learn that Emerson himself used the term only twice in his complete essays and never in his poetry, sermons, or journals. "The Over-Soul" serves as the title of the ninth essay in the *First Series* and occurs in a passage within that essay. He did not employ the term until 1840 (the year of the composition of the essay), at which time the main lines of his philosophy had already been established. Yet in spite of Emerson's own lack of emphasis upon the word, scholarship has adopted it as the focal point and epitomizing metaphor of the Transcendental ontology. . . .

Although the word is a handy one for labeling Emerson's thought, it is also dangerous, not only because it implies an accent that Emerson never had but also because it leads to fruitless speculation. There is little point in arguing about the source of the term, as Harrison, Christy, and Carpenter have done. More important, accepting the concept of the Over-Soul as the main expression of Emerson's thought imparts an unnecessary vagueness to him—the very aura that one tries to overcome in interpreting him.

What is the actual meaning of *Over-Soul*, and what is its place in the Emersonian system? It must be understood in its proper perspective as only a small part of the whole picture, as a single concept which together with other equally important concepts reveals a basic insight into Emerson's idea of God and man. An examination of the only passage in which the word appears yields information regarding his own usage. He writes:

> The Supreme Critic on the errors of the past and the present, and the only prophet of that which must be, is that great nature in which we rest as the earth lies in the soft arms of the atmosphere; that Unity, that Over-Soul, within which every man's particular being is contained and made one with all other; that common heart of which all sincere conversation is the worship, to which all right

action is submission; that overpowering reality which confutes our tricks and talents, and constrains every one to pass for what he is, and to speak from his character and not from his tongue, and which evermore tends to pass into our thought and hand and become wisdom and virtue and power and beauty. We live in succession, in division, in parts, in particles. Meantime within man is the soul of the whole; the wise silence; the universal beauty, to which every part and particle is equally related; the eternal ONE.

There is little doubt that *Over-Soul* is a synonym among other synonyms for God. *Supreme Critic, prophet, wise silence,* and *universal beauty,* for example, are diverse ways of designating the deity. However, each of these synonyms is specialized and says something specific about the Emersonian divinity. If Emerson wishes to make a general statement about God he uses a general term, such as *deity* or *divinity* or even *being* or *essence.* Sometimes he is ambiguous and will employ *spirit* or *soul,* which can mean either *universal* or *individual* spirit and soul, depending upon the context. The underlying difficulty is in Emerson's insistence upon a "panentheistic" view of deity, which understands God as both transcendent and immanent, as inhabiting—in fact, constituting—the universe yet also existing (nonspatially) "outside" it. When terms like *soul* or *spirit* fail to convey enough of his intended meaning, Emerson's strategy is to turn to analogy and a succession of semipoetic synonyms which will appeal to the imagination as well as to the reason of the reader.

Emerson's struggle to communicate his experience of God in the passage cited is indicated by the wealth of synonyms. Examining *Over-Soul* in relation to the other terms, one discovers that it has three fairly distinct connotations. First, it can be understood in the sense of "over-the-soul," as representing a quantitative contrast to the individual soul, since it is more than and therefore greater than the individual soul which man possesses. Thus the individual soul responds to the "that great nature," to "the overpowering reality" somehow outside of itself. Second, the Over-Soul is the "super-soul" (the Germans, if they translate it at all, render *Over-Soul* as *Überseele,* thereby giving the *super-soul* connotation), which indicates a qualitative difference. The Over-Soul is greater than the individual soul because it is not infected by the material qualities of mortality. In its purity and absoluteness, it stands as the model and ultimate goal of the individual soul. The idea corresponds to the Neo-Platonic view of the *One* as first member of the divine triad, through which all emanations begin, and Emerson reveals his indebtedness to that view by referring to "the eternal ONE" as the culminating synonym of the passage. Third, Over-Soul means *general soul,* the all-pervading soul, the principle of divine immanence in man and the world. In spite of the differences in quantity and quality between the individual soul and the universal soul, they are the same in origin and ultimate destination. Emerson's concern is to inform the individual of his present godliness and thus aid him in assimilating his soul to God. His emphasis is therefore on the "Unity" and the "common heart" which man can now experience. Through the word *Over-Soul*, then, Emerson attempts to say that 1) God is different from and more than worldly existence (transcendence); 2) God pervades and forms worldly existence (immanence); 3) man can become one with God even in worldly existence simply by realizing his own divine potential (unity). *Over-Soul* emerges as an imaginative name which combines two aspects of the divine nature, usually thought of as mutually exclusive, while inviting man to share in them.

Far from developing a doctrine of the Over-Soul, Emerson used the word as a description among others for a troublesome, even paradoxical series of concepts about God and man that he explained, both in earlier and later essays, in other terms. As the term *Over-Soul* stands, it is neither very clear nor very valuable as a representative label. If we continue to use it as a convenient catch-all for Emerson's brand of Transcendentalism, we should be aware that we are radically oversimplifying and at once obscuring his thought.

From "The Over-Rated 'Over-Soul,' " *American Literature,* 36 (March 1964), 65-68.

WALTER BLAIR and CLARENCE FAUST

Emerson's Literary Method—the Essay "Art"

THIS PASSAGE [in the *Republic* about the "twice bisected line"] deserves careful study, since Emerson saw it as a key to Platonism, as a key, moreover, representing the range of human knowledge and indicating its kinds. The fundamental division in the line here described—the first bisection—is between the visible world, or the objects of sensation, and the intelligible world. Objects in the realm of sense may again be distinguished as "images, that is both shadows and reflections" of things, on the one hand, and "the objects of these images, that is, plants, animals, and the works of art and nature," on the other hand. And as the visible world may be divided into the realm of physical objects and the realm of the reflections of these objects, so the intelligible world may be divided into the realm of absolute truth and the realm of its reflections in the opinions and hypotheses of men. "To these four sections," adds Emerson, "the four operations of the soul correspond—conjecture, faith, understanding, reason." The line described, then, may be represented as in the accompanying diagram.

INTELLIGIBLE WORLD	{ Truths	[Reason]
	{ Opinions, hypotheses	[Understanding]
VISIBLE WORLD	{ Objects (plants, animals, works of art and nature)	[Faith]
	{ Images (shadows and reflections)	[Conjecture]

Such a set of concepts, Emerson believed, shaped Plato's thinking and the natural and organic expression of it. "Things are knowable," he conceived of the Greek as saying. "They are knowable," Emerson continued, "because being from one, things correspond. There is a scale; and the correspondence of heaven to earth, of matter to mind, of the part to the whole, is our guide." The mind, Emerson explains, is urged to range up this scale—"to ask for one cause of many effects; then for the cause of that; and again the cause, diving still into the profound: self-assured that it shall arrive at an absolute and sufficient one—a one that shall be all." It is also forced to move down the scale: "Urged by an opposite necessity, the mind turns from the one to that which is not one, but other or many; from cause to effect; and affirms the necessary existence of variety, the self-existence of both, as each is involved in the other." "Action," "the power of nature," likewise "tends directly backwards to diversity. . . . Nature is the manifold.". . .

The essay "Art" follows a pattern suggested in Emerson's explanation of "the power and charm" of Plato—"the sea-shore, sea seen from shore, shore seen from sea"—a systematic consideration of the points of view from which related subjects may be viewed. For paragraphs 1-3 of Emerson's essay deal with the causes of Art (the Artists); paragraphs 4-10, with the effects of Art (on the Beholders); paragraphs 11-13 with Art itself. There is also an integrated consideration, first, of Art detached from utility and later of Art with utility.

The first paragraph in section 1—on the Artists—starts with a series of eliminations, It considers, first, all acts of the soul; then only those which result in useful and fine arts; then only the fine arts, in which "not imitation but creation is the aim." Such creation is accomplished, says the author, by an omission from the work of art—of "the details, the prose of nature." The explanation of this omission is stated in terms of the aim or the end of the Artist—to "give the suggestion of a fairer creation than we know" and to give us "only the spirit and splendor." Thus, progressively, the artist, as an active agent, is described as giving the viewer an intimation of splendor, then splendor itself—successive steps on the ladder of comprehension.

Having noticed, in the first half of the paragraph, the artist as active on that which is below him in the scale—manipulating the details of nature and influencing other men—Emerson, in the second half of the paragraph, turns to the artist as passive—receiving a knowledge of that which is above him on the scale. This knowledge is considered progressively. At first it is spoken of as if it belonged to the artist alone: "He should know that the landscape has beauty for his eye because it expresses a thought which is to him good." Then Emerson mentions knowledge of the cause on the scale above both the artist and the object depicted and therefore affecting both of them: the thought is good to the artist "because the same power which sees through his eyes is seen in that spectacle"; and therefore the artist values "the expression of nature and not nature itself" and exalts "in his copy the features that please him." The paragraph concludes with a similar consideration of the artist's relation to human, as compared with natural, subjects. In portraying a man, as in portraying a landscape, the artist must depict "the character and not the features" and he must realize, furthermore, that the appearance of his subject is merely "an imperfect picture or likeness" of that which seeks expression in both painter and subject— "the aspiring original within."

Paragraph 1, then, after its initial eliminations, has done much to show a noteworthy similarity between the artist, the scene he depicts, the human figure he portrays, and the work of art: all of these, though distinguishable, are alike in that they express that which is above them on the scale of being. Paragraph 2 moves toward a unity which eliminates distinctions, showing that, lighted by the "higher illumination" which characterizes all spiritual activity, the differences between artist, human subject, and landscape, between work of art and spirit, disappear. For "what is man," asks Emerson, but nature's work of art, "nature's finest success in self-explication?" And what is man's expression and his love of both his own and nature's expression but "a still finer success"—everything irrelevant left out—"the spirit or moral . . . contracted into a musical word, or the most cunning stroke of the pencil?" With the statement of the likeness of the landscape, man, and man's art as expressions of nature, the examination of the artist, both passive and active, in his relation to the eternal forces operative in his work, is completed.

Since this is only one of the relations in which the artist may be viewed, Emerson, after exhausting his consideration of it, is constrained to "reverse Jove's coin." "But," paragraph 3 therefore begins, "the artist must employ *the symbols in use in his day and nation* to convey his enlarged sense to his fellow men. . . ." The words which we have italicized show that now, having related the artist to that which is timeless, the balanced author is preparing to relate him to his time. The sentence quoted shows the artist actively manipulating contemporary symbols; shortly, however, "the Genius of the Hour"—that above the artist on the scale—is shown becoming the active force. And, says Emerson, "as far as the spiritual character of the period overpowers the artist and finds expression in his work, so far it will retain a certain grandeur, and will represent to future beholders the Unknown, the Inevitable, the Divine." The movement of the consideration of both the time spirit and the artist at this point is clearly in the direction of unity, since the timeless has united with the timely and the artist, willingly or unwillingly, has become the instrument of both. Hence works of art are seen to have value as history, denoting as they do, "the height of the human soul in that hour, and . . . sprung from a necessity as deep as the world." As the section on the Artists ends, therefore, the subject (whether landscape or man), the time or timeless spirit, and the artist (human, subhuman, or divine) have all been seen as uniting to collaborate in "the portrait of that fate, perfect and beautiful, according to whose ordinations all beings advance to their beatitude."

In the next seven paragraphs, as has been suggested, the Beholders of Art, heretofore only briefly mentioned, are considered. Again Emerson starts with the utmost separation and then, by a series of steps, moves toward unity. He begins by picturing us, blind to the beauty in which we are immersed, capable only of an infant-like trance. Then an artist of superior powers detaches for us "one object from the embarrassing variety," and, since "the object has its roots in central nature," it "may of course be so exhibited to us as to represent the world." This is the initiatory step of art in educating the perception of beauty. Presently another step is taken; we have our attention concentrated upon some other object, this time in nature itself, and from both works of art and natural objects "we learn at last the immensity of the world, the opulence of human nature, which can run out to infinitude in any direction." In this way we learn variety. But we also learn that all things have likenesses and that "the excellence of all things is one."

But even after describing this progress, Emerson may still say that painting and sculpture are merely initial (par. 5). Going beyond such teachings, they eventually so open the eyes of the beholder that he sees "the eternal picture which nature paints"—yes, achieving even deeper insight, the beholder comprehends (with his highest faculty, the Reason) the Beauty and Truth which breathe through nature. This experience of the art is explained (in pars. 7-10) by "the reference of all production at last to an aboriginal Power." We perceive the beautiful only when we "carry it with us," that is, when the power which operates through the artist also operates in the beholder of his work. The work of a genius seems, then, not "a stranger" or "a foreign wonder," but "familiar, simple, a home-speaking countenance . . . as if one should meet a friend." In short, artist and beholder are unified in their experience of a power expressing itself in both. And now, gifted with such insight, the beholder finds that even the greatest pictures wrought by geniuses express "the old, eternal fact" which they have "met already in so many forms." Though this is one of the highest possible reaches of the section, Emerson again announces (par. 10) that "the arts . . . are but initial"; for, even when so experienced they are mere "tokens of the everlasting effort to produce," unnaturally separated from the practical and the moral. "There is a higher work for Art than the arts. They are abortive births of an imperfect or vitiated instinct. . . . Nothing less than the creation of man and nature is Art's end." A painter or sculptor, therefore, eventually should be impatient of anything less than this high achievement; and the beholder should be awakened by Art not only to comprehension but also to this highest sort of artistic creation:

> Art should exhilarate, and throw down the walls of circumstance on every side, awakening in the beholder the same sense of universal relation and power which the work evinced in the artist, and its highest effect is to make new artists.

In this way, Art, earlier seen as valuable for the beholder because it furnished insight he himself could not achieve, now comes to be seen as giving the beholder insights equal to those of the artist. And these insights have acquainted the beholder with the highest reaches of artistic achievement and with the need for a unification of art with action and life.

In the first section, it has been suggested, the Artist, seen at first as detached, has been seen at the end achieving unity; in the second section the Beholder moves from similar detachment to similar unity. Not surprisingly, therefore, the third section (pars. 11-13) starts with the detachment of the arts from one another and from nature and ends with their unification among themselves and with nature. Particular arts—first sculpture, then painting, then music—are seen to be below Nature and separated from it—in the lowest realm of the scale of being among shadows and reflections.[1] These appear imperfect "before that new activity which needs to roll through all things"—an activity which has been mentioned, in another connection, at the end of the second section—an activity, moreover, which is to be the unifying force in this section. "A true announcement of the law of creation," says Emerson, "if a man were found worthy to declare it, would carry art [from the level of mere images] into the kingdom of nature, and destroy its separate and contrasted existence." Art is also to be criticized, it appears in this section, when it separates itself from utility—"This division . . . the laws of nature do not permit." When art tends "to detach the beautiful from the useful," Emerson notes (par. 13), it is also detached from its creators:

> The art that thus separates is itself first separated. Art must not be a superficial talent, but must begin farther back in man. Now men do not see nature to be beautiful, and they go to make a statue which shall be. They abhor men as tasteless, dull, and inconvertible, and console themselves with color-bags and blocks of marble. . . . They eat and drink, that they may afterwards execute the ideal. Thus art is vilified . . . it stands in the imagination as somewhat contrary to nature, and struck with death from the first.

Such separation, in the transcendental system, may be remedied by uniting action and insight on a higher level. "Would it not be better," the author therefore asks, "to begin higher up, . . . to serve the ideal in eating and drinking, in drawing the breath, and in the functions of life? Beauty must come back to the useful arts, and the distinction between the fine and the useful arts be forgotten." "Proceeding from a religious heart," genius may cause Art to serve the one above even man—may "raise *to a divine use* the railroad, the insurance office, the joint-stock company; our law, our primary assemblies, our commerce, the galvanic battery, the electric jar, the prism, and the chemist's retort. . . ."[2]

Each of the three topics related to Art—the Artist, the Beholder, and Art—now having been treated in relationship to one another, to the whole range of the scale, and to the comprehension of them by varying faculties, the essay may be said to have "united to an object the notion which belongs to it," and may therefore properly conclude.

From "Emerson's Literary Method," *Modern Philology*, 42 (Nov. 1944), 79-95.

1. In the diagram above, in accordance with the passage in [Emerson's essay] "Plato," we have shown works of art in the realm of Objects on the scale of being. But in the sense of this passage they are to be considered imperfect copies or images of objects. In the Emersonian system this involves no inconsistency, since the system provides for both ways of viewing such works.

2. The italics here and in other quotations are ours. The semicolon distinguishes the purely commercial creations of man from those which, though commercial, are the result of intellectual investigation and scientific experimentation.

F. O. MATTHIESSEN

The Democratic Core of *Representative Men*

WHAT EMERSON conceived to be 'the symbols in use in his day and nation,' which he must use in turn if he was to express the meaning of its life, can be read most clearly in *Representative Men*. Notwithstanding his satisfaction in his New England setting, he repeatedly declared that nature must be humanized, that its beauty 'must always seem unreal and mocking, until the landscape has human figures that are as good as itself.' His selection of such figures—Plato, Swedenborg, Montaigne, Shakespeare, Napoleon, Goethe—is by itself ample evidence of his freedom from any restrictions of nationalism. He knew that an American renaissance needed the encouragement of great writers and thinkers. His timelessness took for granted his country's immediate share in the whole cultural heritage.

One inevitable stimulus to the form of this book was Carlyle's *Heroes and Hero-Worship* (1841). But even before that appeared, Emerson had reached his own position that 'there is properly no history, only biography,' a position that Thoreau, in his confidence, carried to the point of saying, 'Biography, too, is liable to the same objection; it should be autobiography.' Carlyle's book was more than a stimulus: it provided the assumptions against which Emerson made a quiet but fundamental counterstatement. The difference between the titles is significant. 'Great men,' said Emerson, 'the word is injurious'; and his grounds for objection to Carlyle were both religious and social. The source of his own title was probably Swedenborg, whom he celebrated for daring to take the last and boldest step of genius, to provide a theory of interpretation for the meaning of existence. Emerson quoted triumphant evidence of this from *The Animal Kingdom:* 'In our doctrine of Representations and Correspondences we shall treat of both these symbolical and typical resemblances, and of the astonishing things which occur, I will not say in the living body only, but throughout nature, and which correspond so entirely to supreme and spiritual things that one would swear that the physical world was purely symbolical of the spiritual world.' Swedenborg's correspondences were in harmonious keeping with Emerson's belief that what made one man more representative than another was the degree to which he was a receptive channel for the superincumbent spirit. Emerson held Carlyle's greatest blemish to be his inadequate understanding of spirituality. As Henry

James, Sr. phrased it: 'Moral force was the deity of Carlyle's unscrupulous worship,—the force of unprincipled, irresponsible will.' As a result he had glorified the strong men of history, in a sequence that devolved from Odin to Cromwell to Frederick of Prussia, and thus helped prepare the way for our contemporary fatal worship of force. Though Emerson did not phrase himself with James' terseness, he grew to realize the drastic importance of Carlyle's defect.

What Emerson wanted to say was that 'no individual was great, except through the general.' He could go so far as to speak of the 'inflamed individualism' that separated the man of power from the mass of his fellows. But he had not gone far enough to satisfy himself. As soon as he had sent *Representative Men* to press, he regretted that 'many after thoughts, as usual . . . come just a little too late; and my new book seems to lose all value from their omission. Plainly one is the justice that should have been done to the unexpressed greatness of the common farmer and laborer.' . . .

In [Theodore] Parker's solid if somewhat naive objections [to history as "dramatic pageants"] we come to the democratic core of New England transcendentalism. For Parker believed that an American historian must write in the interest of mankind, in the spirit of the nineteenth century. He must be occupied with the growth of institutions, not with glamorous spectacles. 'He must tell us of the social state of the people, the relation of the cultivator to the soil, the relation of class to class. It is well to know what songs the peasant sung; what prayers he prayed; what food he ate; what tools he wrought with; what tax he paid; how he stood connected with the soil; how he was brought to war; and what weapons armed him for the fight.'

Through this view of history Emerson's age found its myth. . . .

Emerson penetrated to the heart of this myth in his conception (1846) of 'the central man,' the creative source of all vitality. He imagined himself in talk with him, and that the voice of the central man was that of Socrates. 'Then the discourse changes, and the man, and we see the face and hear the tones of Shakespeare . . . A change again, and the countenance of our companion is youthful and beardless, he talks of form and color and the riches of design; it is the face of the painter Raffaelle.' Next it is Michel Angelo, then Dante, afterwards Jesus: 'And so it appears that these great secular personalities were only expressions of his face chasing each other like the rack of clouds.' The Orphic poet who spoke at the end of *Nature* had voiced a kindred parable of the continual renewal of man's heroic energy. Emerson felt that in *Representative Men* he had only managed to suggest this under a few shadowy guises. Looking back at this book a dozen years later, he said that he had sensed when writing it that Jesus was the 'Representative Man' whom he ought to sketch, but that he had not felt equal to the task. . . .

Where he was at his best in *Representative Men* was in translating Plato into Concord, in giving a portrait of ·Socrates as a 'plain old uncle . . . with his great ears, an immense talker,' 'what our country-people call *an old one.*' Emerson's concern in this book with man's common nature also gave him an insight into the value of tradition that we would hardly expect from him. Elsewhere, as in 'Self-Reliance,' he often said, 'Where is the master who could have taught Shakespeare? . . . Every great man is a unique.' But here he saw that 'the rude warm blood of the living England circulated in the play, as in street-ballads.' He went even farther and declared: 'What is best written or done by genius in the world, was no man's work, but came by wide social labor, when a thousand wrought like one, sharing the same impulse.' Unhappily Emerson . . . could not make much out of that perception. The 'genius of humanity' that he announced to be his real subject could become very amorphous, most devastatingly so in his vague treatment of his modern figures, Napoleon and Goethe. It was no accident that his passage on the different incarnations of 'the central man' ended with these sentences: 'Then all will subside, and I find myself alone. I dreamed and did not know my dreams.'

From *American Renaissance: Art and Expression in the Age of Emerson and Whitman* (New York: Oxford Univ. Press, 1941), pp. 631-35.

FREDERIC IVES CARPENTER

Orientalism in *The Conduct of Life*

DURING THE general period from 1850 to 1860 Emerson was widely interested in Oriental literature in every way. The depth of this interest is only discovered by a close reading of his essays on *The Conduct of Life*.

This volume was published in 1860, when Emerson was fifty-seven, and constitutes logically the conclusion and fulfilment of his life work. It contains his most mature wisdom. It rounds out the series of essays that he had begun with *Nature* in 1836. And he introduces this last volume significantly with his essay on "Fate", and concludes it with that on "Illusions". These two deal most directly and fully with Oriental ideas, and are filled with quotations from the Orient, woven in to illustrate the very central current of the thought. Indian fables develop the Mohammedan feeling for Fatalism, and Persian verses help to bring out the Hindu conception of Illusion. Between these terminal essays, too, are numerous Oriental quotations and ideas, especially in the discussions of "Worship" and "Beauty". This final book is shot through with the colors of Oriental thought.

But Emerson did not merely accept Oriental ideas; he transmuted them. He used them to illustrate and give substance to his own thought. His essay on "Fate" argues to the conclusion that the fatal laws of the world may also be turned to man's advantage, once they are realized and accepted. And this whole essay is capped by the succeeding essay on "Power", which develops the idea of Freedom, and urges it much more conclusively. Finally, the closing essay on "Illusions" suggests the beneficent force of the illusions of the world, by the understanding of which man may gain a new sight of "the gods sitting there on their thrones."

This ability to interpret Oriental ideas in his own way Emerson kept throughout the rest of his life.

From *Emerson and Asia* (Cambridge, Mass.: Harvard Univ. Press, 1930), pp. 23-24.

SEYMOUR L. GROSS

Emerson and Poetry

FIRST OF ALL, Emerson's theory, which has been termed "organic," if taken without important qualifications, is aesthetically impossible; and, secondly, Emerson in his poetry does seem to be conscious of his theoretic dicta,. which paradoxically enough, cause his poetry to be "inorganic." Emerson's theory of art, like almost everything he wrote, was conditioned by a passionate desire to affirm order in the universe. Once he was metaphysically certain of the basic unity of all experience, each aspect of it with which he dealt had in order to be "true" to be related to the basic nature of the world as he understood it. But unfortunately this compulsion was all too often sheer emotionalism: his feelings rather than his rational faculties determined his statements. But since "feelings" are almost by definition vacillating, it follows that the statements which stem from these feelings can have no more stability than that which motivates them: hence the multitude of contradictions that one finds in Emerson's works. Furthermore, there is the ambivalence of the man himself. He constantly struggled to lift himself from the thrilling apperception of the thing itself (which he did not trust) to a mystical awareness of its spirit. The English metaphysical poets managed to achieve this movement repeatedly, but Emerson could not. Herbert and Donne, unlike Emerson, are rationalists in their poetry and give the semblance of inductive discovery within the poem; Emerson begins with the discovery and is heedless of the process by which discovery is reached. Thus Donne and Herbert give us the density of real experience, while Emerson gives us only the conclusions.

Emerson's ambivalence shows itself in the many statements he makes about art. He seemed to be torn between a belief that art was illusion and that art was the highest possible human activity. In the opening section of *Nature* he relegates art to an almost oriental nothingness. In speaking of the artist he says, "But his operations taken together are so insignificant, a little chipping, baking, patching, and washing, that in an impression so grand as that of the world on the human mind, they do not vary the result." This belittlement of the artist is the perverted result of Emerson's belief that the world is better and more wonderful than anything that can be done with it. To concede that the artist could "vary the result" would have been for Emerson a tacit admission that the world was not the perfect creation he so zealously but naively believed it to be.

But in "The American Scholar" of the following year Emerson shifts his ground. He seems to realize that experience is, at least in its superficial aspect, formless; that it is the artist who must find and impart the meaning of life, which for most other men has been obfuscated by the egocentric business of living. "The theory of books is noble. The scholar of the first age received into him the world around; brooded thereupon; gave it the new arrangement of his own mind, and uttered it again. It came into him life; it went out from him truth. . . . It came to him business; it went from him poetry." Here, then, the artist is placed in a new perspective: experience is an endless mass of variety, which, when passed through the alembic of the artist, emerges as truth.

But how precisely was this to be accomplished? Once again Emerson wavers. Selection, the technical foundation of art, recommends itself to Emerson, but when he does accept it, it is with decided misgivings. In his essay *Art* he writes: "The virtue of art lies in detachment, in sequestering one object from the embarrassing variety. Until one thing comes out from the connection of things, there can be enjoyment, contemplation but no thought." But several pages later Emerson seems to be wondering whether this detachment is not after all a violation of the "Whole." All works of art should not be detached, but extempore performances." If one may guess at the thought process which caused these two contradictory statements, it might go something like this: The artist in order to convert life into truth must wrench an object out of its experiential context; but the very act of wrenching is apparently artificial, unreal, and consequently a lie. This paradox Emerson solved for himself by means of the symbol. "Every natural fact is a symbol of some spiritual fact. Every appearance in nature corresponds to some state of mind, and that state of mind can only be described by presenting that natural appearance as its picture."

Although Emerson quite correctly realizes that abstractions can be expressed only in terms of concrete images, he makes the crucial mistake of assuming that these natural facts have this power intrinsically: "This power is in the image because this power is in Nature." But this is obviously begging an important question. It is the poet who, after comprehending the experience with which he deals, makes the symbol serve as the vehicle of description and definition. . . .

But for Emerson the organic roots of the symbol go deeper than the fact that natural objects symbolize spiritual truths. "Parts of speech are metaphors, because the whole of nature is a metaphor of the human mind." But, for all his faith in the power of the symbol to express the fact and its spiritual conterpart concurrently, he was constantly leaving the symbol behind for the superficial solidity of direct statement. In a real sense he did not trust the symbol, and his distrust arose from his technical inability to manipulate a basically unified metaphor. It is one thing to say that there is no fact in nature which does not carry the whole sense of nature, but it is something quite different to make it work in a poem. This technical inadequacy, which his theory sanctions, causes him to introduce a symbol into his verse, drop it, and go darting after another with irritating abandon. [F. O.] Matthiessen is very much to the point when he says, "though he talked about the unexampled resources of metaphor and symbol, his staple device was analogy." Certainly, Emerson's belief in the symbol's innate power tò convey the "whole sense of nature" points more to the use of analogy than symbol. In reading Emerson's poetry one receives the feeling of momentary illustration more than that of the permanent awareness of a symbol fully conceived and exploited. Further, as the poems of Donne and Crashaw abundantly show, the symbol is capable of defining states of feeling, while analogy, with its brief dazzle, is too feeble to catch the density of attitude. To be convinced one need only compare Emerson's "Initial Love" with Donne's "Lover's Infiniteness."

The relationship between beauty and art Emerson discusses many times, but perhaps nowhere so poignantly as in *Nature*. . . . In short, the artist is filled with the beauty of nature, which fullness causes him to express its beauty in microcosm, which in turn suggests its beauty in macrocosm.

But this beauty signified to Emerson the moral as well as the aesthetic, or rather the single identity of both. He says in the same essay, "Beauty is the mark God sets upon virtue," and again, "Truth, and goodness, and beauty are but different faces of the same All." Emerson wanted desperately to believe this naive, romantic concept, but even on the very same page he says, "No reason can be asked or given why the soul seeks beauty." This, of course, poses a problem. For if it is incomprehensible why the soul seeks beauty, and beauty is truth, then it is equally incomprehensible why the soul seeks truth; thus man becomes a subrational creature unable to understand why he strives to attain that which will presumably make him free. Certainly Emerson would be aghast at the implications of his own statements. . . . Emerson, whether he would or not, was sensitive to the beauty of things irrespective of their "spiritual suggestion"; but once having placed his philosophic faith in the romantic creed, he is tossed ambivalently from the sturdy wall of what he felt to the nebulous wall of what he wished to feel. . . .

The perfectness of nature also led Emerson to the criterion by which poetic excellence is to be judged. "For poetry was all written before time was, and whenever we are so finely organized that we can penetrate into that region where the air is all music, we hear those primal warblings and attempt to write them down, but we lose ever and anon a word or a verse and substitute something of our own, and thus miswrite the poem." Nature, then, is to be the eternal standard by which art is to be judged. But how is nature to be ascertained? Emerson's prescription is as terrifying as is any prescription which raises man's instincts above his rational capacities: "The lover of nature is he whose inward and outward senses are still truly adjusted to each other; who has retained the spirit of infancy even unto the era of manhood." This Wordsworthian faith Emerson carries to even more grotesque extremes in his essay *History*: "The idiot, the Indian, the child and unschooled farmer's boy stand nearer to the light by which nature is to be read, than the dissecter or the antiquary." This is faith in the self-reliance of the dog, not the man. How or why the idiot and the ignorant boy are able to pierce the density of experience, when the rational dissecter cannot, is beyond comprehension; in fact it is demonstrably false. This is not to say that the dissecter can solve the riddle of nature, but rather that if that part of us which distinguishes us from beasts cannot arrive at truth, certainly that part of us which we have in common with them cannot.

Emerson's doctrine of inspiration is but the other side of his belief that the simple mind can best read nature. The poet has just such a simple mind in the Emerson scheme. The poet in some way which is undiscoverable becomes intoxicated with inspiration, and "That is the best part of each writer which has nothing private in it; that which he does not know." That is, the poet is presumably able to describe and delineate an experience which he himself does not understand. Strange as it may seem, this is precisely what Emerson believes: "The universal nature, too strong for the petty nature of the bard, sits on his neck and writes through his hand; so that when he seems to vent a mere caprice and wild romance, the issue is an exact allegory." The poet, then, is a mystified middleman, who, through God's gift, is able to pass on the truths of nature to those less gifted. Not only is poetry not a rational process, as we understand the term, it is the product of a divine madness. "The poet knows that he speaks adequately then only when he speaks somewhat wildly . . . not with the intellect used as an organ, but with the intellect released from all service . . . with the intellect inebriated by nectar." How such emotionalism is able to reshape experience into coherent, communicable form is difficult to conceive.

Perhaps Emerson's reaction to his intellectual heritage with its Puritanical and, to a lesser extent, Unitarian rigidity of thought drove him to the outrageous belief that "our spontaneous action is always best." This idea is carried over to his literary theory. "The moment our discourse rises above the ground line of facts and is inflamed with passion or exalted thought, it clothes itself in images. . . . This imagery is spontaneous." The poetic process is thus further removed from the realm of the rational: not only is the source of the creative process outside the poet's understanding, but so is the very process itself. It is difficult to imagine how Emerson found "spontaneity" in the wrenched, exciting imagery of the metaphysical poets whom he so admired. Indeed, the use of radical imagery in such a poem of his as "Spiritual Laws" betokens more a self-conscious, though unsuccessful, drawing together of incongruous elements and a balancing of antithetical images than any spontaneous emission.

Although Emerson was drawn to the image because he felt that only it could hold language at once to the senses and the intellect, he was decidedly uncomfortable with only the ontological reality: "The details, the prose of nature he [the poet] should omit and give us only the spirit and the splendor." Since for Emerson the primary use of the fact is low, he recklessly leaves it behind in his attempts to grasp the nebulae of spirit; consequently the movement of his verse is fuzzy and unmotivated. His leaps for "the constant fact of life" often rip up the realistic foundations of his image, and we are left in a blurry transcendental haze without knowing how or why we got there.

Perhaps nowhere in Emerson's theory of poetry does his compulsion to relate everything to an organic whole manifest itself so ludicrously as in his theory of meters. He did not see that meter is essentially a tool with which the poet shapes and controls his material, that its superficial artificiality serves the higher function of form. But, since Emerson's philosophical edifice had no readily available niche into which such artificiality could be made to fit, he invented one. "Meter begins with the pulse beat, and the length of lines in poems and songs is determined by the inhalation and exhalation of the lungs."

On first glance, it seems one of the most perplexing of paradoxes that such an enthusiastic devotee of the organic principle in art could so seldom write a poem that holds together. But when we consider the chaotic implications of his theory, we are surprised that one or two of his poems are successful. . . .

"Each and All," a much admired poem among Emersonians, suffers from such lack of form and transition. The poem opens with a number of particularized examples of the usually unperceived interlocking nature of experience: a scarecrow in the field does not know that you are looking at it; a heifer lows, uncaring and unknowing that its lowing charms a human ear; a sexton does not know that the music of his bells has made Napoleon stop to listen; nor does man know how the example of his life has helped his neighbor's creed. But suddenly there is inserted in lines eleven and twelve the abrupt generalized statement; "All are needed by each one; / Nothing is fair or good alone." These lines, coming without any transition from the particularized suggestiveness of the previous lines, startle us. The symbolic construct of the specific examples is swept away in the clipped meter of the expositional aphorism. The pattern of the first ten lines, that of ascending movement from inanimate to animal to man to spirit, is forced into the direct statement, and the poignancy of concrete awareness is thoroughly effaced.

We are then introduced to the poet, who, as direct participant, is to carry forward the theme that all are needed by each one. But, at this point, the poem, really begins anew. We are able to carry to it only the abstract, generalized statement, which acts with no more force than a sort of thesis sentence.

> I thought the sparrow's note from heaven,
> Singing at dawn on the alder bough.
> I brought him home, in his nest, at even;
> He sings the song, but it cheers not now,
> For I did not bring home the river and sky;—
> He sang to my ear,—they sang to my eye.

The meaning is clear. The poet found beauty in the sparrow's note only when the bird was part of its natural surroundings; when brought to the poet's home it still sings, but it no longer pleases: it has lost its relationship to totality. Beauty, then, is in the thing connected, not in the thing isolated. Symbols are seemingly set up for this dichotomy: the ear or sound for isolation, the eye or sight for connection. But in the next section of the poem these symbols are jumbled.

> The delicate shells lay on the shore;
> The bubbles of the latest wave
> Fresh pearls to their enamel gave,
> And the bellowing of the savage sea
> Greeted their safe escape to me.
> I wiped away the weeds and foam,
> I fetched my sea-born treasures home;
> But the poor, unsightly, noisome things
> Had left their beauty on the shore
> With the sun and the sand and the wild uproar.

In this section sound is represented as part of the totality: "the sun and the sand and the wild uproar" sing both to the eye and the ear. This hasty dropping of the symbols indicates a certain confusion in the poet's mind, even more clearly seen in the next section.

To this point we are to see that beauty is real only in its natural totality. In the following lines the poet deals with something quite different, unintentionally changing the emphasis:

> The lover watched his graceful maid,
> As 'mid the virgin train she strayed,
> Nor knew her beauty's best attire
> Was woven still by the snow-white choir.
> At last she came to his hermitage,
> Like the birds from the woodlands to the cage;—
> The gay enchantment was undone,
> A gentle wife but fairy none.

This is almost ridiculous. The young woman's natural totality is arbitrary, lacking the "necessity" that the river and the sky have for the sparrow or the sun, sand, and ocean for the seashell. The virgin train is proper to her only while she is a snow-white virgin. To feel cheated that she is no fairy, but only a gentle wife, is to equate peevishly the fluctuating contexts of human beings with the fixed contexts of natural objects; the maid is not isolated, as were the shell and sparrow; for she has exchanged one perfectly natural state for another, virginity for marriage. Therefore, the disillusionment of this section is motivated by an unreasonably romantic turn of mind, the previous two by moral awareness. What is significant is that all three are presented as if identically motivated.

To this point the poem has dealt unsuccessfully with the necessity of totality to beauty. But Emerson's belief that poetry must ascend to the most spiritual of heights, no matter how, causes his poem to carom off into a direction completely unprepared for.

> Then I said, 'I covet truth;
> Beauty is unripe childhood's cheat;
> I leave it behind with the games of youth:'—
> As I spoke, beneath my feet
> The ground-pine curled its pretty wreath,
> Running over the club-moss burrs;
> I inhaled the violet's breath;
> Around me stood the oaks and firs;
> Pine-cones and acorns lay on the ground;
> Over me soared the eternal sky,
> Full of light and of deity;
> Again I say, again I heard,
> The rolling river, the morning bird;—
> Beauty through my senses stole;
> I yielded myself to the perfect whole.

The poet now rejects beauty and chooses truth. But this is not clear. The "truth" of the poem the poet has already apprehended: nothing is beautiful alone. What truth is he then choosing? Unfortunately, this remains an obscure, abstract choice, meaningless and undefined. But the rejection is but momentary: the poet becomes reaware of the beauty of nature, further realizes that this beauty is truth as well ("full of light and of deity"), and succumbs to the total perfection. The poem has ill prepared us for this "discovery." Until this last section it has been solely concerned with the nature of beauty as beauty; therefore, the ideational leap to this "spiritual truth" is effected without logic, force, or conviction. . . .

"Days" is probably Emerson's finest poetic achievement. If a successful poem is an indication of moral awareness, he must have understood the terrifying paradox of human choice: that in choosing one thing over another we lose forever the good in what we have rejected.

> Daughters of Time, the hypocritic Days,
> Muffled and dumb like barefoot dervishes,
> And marching single in an endless file,
> Bring diadems and fagots in their hands.
> To each they offer gifts after his will,
> Bread, kingdoms, stars, and sky that holds them all.
> I, in my pleached garden, watched the pomp,
> Forgot my morning wishes, hastily
> Took a few herbs and apples, and the Day
> Turned and departed silent. I, too late,
> Under her solemn fillet saw the scorn.

The Days bring gifts which range from brilliant glory (diadems) to those of humble utility (fagots); but the Days can give no indication of relative worth; they are muffled and dumb. Man's free will chooses from amongst the ascending hierarchy of bread, kingdoms, stars, and sky. The poet's morning wishes for stars and sky are forgotten as he watches the pomp, and he innocently chooses the modest growth of his garden. But he has not really forgotten, for his were wishes, not resolutions. This is significant. A resolution presupposes a vice, but a wish presupposes a yearning. The herbs and apples which the poet chooses are not intrinsically evil symbols, but the measure of excellence of a pleached garden. The poet realizes that he has not chosen evil over good, but rather one good over another, though of a lower order. He yearns for the capacity of higher choice while recognizing his fallible humanity. He has but two hands: to clutch for the stars and sky is to drop the herbs and apples. Yet he realizes that in an absolute sense he has chosen wrong, and the perplexity of his innocent guilt, subtly pointed up by the halting rhythm of, "I, too late, / Under her solemn fillet saw the scorn," touches the pain of the paradox. True, the Days do scorn the poet's choice, but it is the scorn that must come to most human beings for being human.

This poem, unlike almost everything else Emerson wrote, is firmly rooted in what he was able to understand. It does not vaporize into a vague, transcendental ether of intuitive feeling. It is above all intensely human. When Emerson left behind him the frantic leaps for superhuman truth and dealt rationally with experience, he managed to achieve such poetic excellence as "Days." But only then.

From "Emerson and Poetry," *The South Atlantic Quarterly,* 54 (Jan. 1955), 82-94.

RICHARD P. ADAMS

Emerson and the Organic Metaphor

LET ME BEGIN by making some distinctions between the organic and the two most important other ways of looking at the universe which were available to Emerson in the 1820's. The first of these was formism, which has descended from Platonic idealism and which is mainly to be found in the humanistic tradition. Younger, but vastly more popular, was mechanism, characteristic of the "new philosophy" of science which had disturbed and then defeated the humanists in the seventeenth century and which has pretty much dominated mass thinking ever since. Because Emerson hated mechanism from the start, his problem was to find some more effective means of fighting it than those used unsuccessfully by the humanists. Like most romantics, he adopted the organic rather than the formistic theory, although he did not emphasize the differences between the two, perhaps because he did not see them very clearly and perhaps partly because he felt that the common antipathy to mechanism was more important. The distinction is none the less real.

When I suggest that Emerson was an organicist, I mean that he did not habitually think of the universe as a copy of ideal reality or form, in the Platonic manner, or as a vast self-regulating machine, in the manner of eighteenth-century scientific rationalists, but that he thought of it as if it were like a living plant or animal. Two crucial differences may be seen between this way of thinking and the others: first, that change, in the tradition of romantic organicism, is a good thing because it implies growth, or the quality of life, which is not inherent in the assumptions of either scientific mechanism or Platonic idealism; second, that organicism is more strongly synthetic than either of the others. A mechanist is inclined to feel that things can be best understood if they are separated into their component parts, and if each observed effect is assigned its proper cause. A formist also is likely to insist on the importance of distinctions, because each prototypical idea, being eternally itself, is different from every other idea. An organicist, however, tends to concentrate, often with a rather mystical air, on the wholeness of the whole, reluctant to analyze at all, maintaining with Wordsworth that "We murder to dissect," . . .

Reluctance to separate things can be a weakness, and romantic writers who use this kind of thinking are sometimes vulnerable to the favorite criticism of humanists, that their treatment blurs the basic distinctions. However, organicism derives its greatest advantages from this same synthetic tendency. Alfred N. Whitehead has sharply criticized the scheme of mechanistic materialism on the ground that it gives "no reason in the nature of things why portions of material should have any physical relations to each other," and he favors "the abandonment of the traditional scientific materialism, and the substitution of an alternative doctrine of organism,"[1] citing the romantic nature poetry of Wordsworth and others as a practical source of ideas for scientists today.

Historically, then, the role of organicism would seem to be that it offers a possible means of transcending the mechanistic difficulty in showing relationships, a problem that humanistic idealism does not solve. The way that organicists have of concentrating on functional relations has in fact proved useful in many practical activities, from architecture to the synthesis of rubber, as well as in the fine arts and in metaphysics.

If there were or could be such a thing as a perfect organicist, Emerson was certainly not one. However, his most eloquent statements of belief are often remarkably similar to some of the best descriptions of the organic theory available today. Let us consider, for example, the following passage by Stephen C. Pepper:

> Organicism . . . is the world hypothesis that stresses the internal relatedness or coherence of things. It is impressed with the manner in which observations at first apparently unconnected turn out to be closely related, and with the fact that as knowledge progresses it becomes more systematized. It conceives the value of our knowledge as proportional to the degree of integration it has attained, and comes to identify value with integration in all spheres. Value in the sphere of knowledge is integration of judgments; in the sphere of ethics, it is integration of acts; in the sphere of art, it is integration of feelings. Finally, it conceives all of these as contained in a total integration of existence or reality.[2]

Organicism, by this account, is not concerned with ideal forms or categorical distinctions, like formism, or with analysis of causes and effects, like mechanism. Its aim is to realize the ultimate organization of all things in a unity which includes them as they are, a harmonious relationship of human experience with all the processes of nature, or the universe.

Now let us compare Emerson's familiar and justly famous passage concerning the influence of nature on the scholar's mind in the Phi Beta Kappa Address of 1837, "The American Scholar":

> Far too as her splendors shine, system on system shooting like rays,

upward, downward, without centre, without circumference,—in the
mass and in the particle, Nature hastens to render account of herself to the mind. Classification begins. To the young mind every
thing is individual, stands by itself. By and by, it finds how to join
two things and see in them one nature; then three, then three
thousand; and so, tyrannized over by its own unifying instinct, it
goes on tying things together, diminishing anomalies, discovering
roots running under ground whereby contrary and remote things
cohere and flower out from one stem. . . . The ambitious soul sits
down before each refractory fact; one after another reduces all
strange constitutions, all new powers, to their class and their law,
and goes on forever to animate the last fibre of organization, the
outskirts of nature, by insight.

Thus to him, to this schoolboy under the bending dome of day,
is suggested that he and it proceed from one root; one is leaf and
one is flower; relation, sympathy, stirring in every vein (I, 85-86).[3]

Here Emerson is obviously in close agreement with the main tenet of
organicism as Pepper defines it, that the important thing to discover is
not causes or archetypal ideas but relatedness, and his account of the
progress of knowledge is the same, that it is a continuous integration of
one fact with another, leading toward a total integration of the universe. He takes pains to repudiate the formistic belief that each fact is a
thing in itself, and he makes it perfectly clear, especially in his final
image, that he derives his formula from the basic metaphor of the living
plant.[4] This metaphor embodies the concept of progressive relatedness
and ultimate unity . . .

"The American Scholar" seems to me in fact the best of Emerson's
efforts to present his whole view in a single work. It is superior to
Nature in many ways, but the important point for this study is that its
consistency of tone and consecutiveness of argument are largely due to
the fact that the organic metaphor is dominant from the first paragraph, which appeals for an American culture offering "something
better than the exertions of mechanical skill," to the last, which calls
on American scholars "to yield that peculiar fruit which each man was
created to bear . . . " (Works, I, 81, 115). The central point, on which
the whole essay depends, is that the social body of humanity is properly "One Man," in contrast to the present state of society, "in which the
members have suffered amputation from the trunk, and strut about so
many walking monsters,—a good finger, a neck, a stomach, an elbow,
but never a man" (I, 82-83). That is, the organic wholeness of humanity
and of individual men has been destroyed by mechanical specialization.
And again . . . mankind is compared to the fingers of a hand, which
ought to cooperate in the functional unity of the organ to which they
belong.

A striking feature of "The American Scholar" is the emphasis repeatedly placed on the principle of change, progression, and originality
implied in the metaphor of the living organism. The scholar, Emerson
insists, cannot be content with merely assimilating other men's ideas; he
must go on to create his own. He must be the publisher of living,
contemporary truth, never merely the parrot of dead thoughts from the
past. The object of knowledge is not a static, absolute ideal but a
growing body, and the scholar who understands its character and his
own "shall look forward to an ever expanding knowledge as to a becoming creator" (I, 86). He will be an original force in a changing
world, which yet has finally a total unity of organization. It is the
business of Man Thinking to understand, and the business of all mankind to act in harmony with the movement toward, this final unity.
The great eloquence of the essay seems to derive largely from the fact
that Emerson for a happy moment forgot the goal in his enthusiasm for
the dynamic quality of the drive itself, the sense of creative activity
resulting from original thinking in terms of the organic metaphor. . . .

The difficulty in the nature of organicism itself is that it contains a
logical contradiction. Its most obvious weakness . . . is the mutual in-
compatibility of . . . its progressive and its ideal categories, that is, its
dynamic and its static aspects. The organicist sees the world in two
ways. In everyday experience it is a various and changing complex of
phenomena, which he believes to be real in spite of the fragmentary and
often irreconcilable appearances which it presents. But at the same time
it is ultimately an integration (or, as Emerson would say, using the term
in its original sense, an "organization") of everything in a unity which is
not temporal, or various, or changing, and in which all fragments are
related and all superficial inconsistencies reconciled. He may be
tempted to suppose that the timeless unity is the real aspect and that
experience seems fragmentary only because of his inability to comprehend the final unity; but he is really neither a dualistic nor a monis-
tic idealist. He believes in the seamless continuity of all things, and he
feels that material and temporal appearances are not false, or different
from the ultimate reality, but parts of it. This reality, of course, does
not consist of norms or patterns but is the single principle of organization that makes creation a universe instead of a multiverse. Stated
crudely, the difficulty lies in believing that the universe really changes,
but that it really does not change, a paradox which disappears in the
image of the living tree but which is hard to resolve in any discursive
treatment of the metaphor and its implications.

Emerson was aware of this problem and acutely conscious of his
inability to solve it, as several passages in his journals and published
works indicate. His best method of treating it was to make the inconsistency itself serve him in the dialectic movement of his thinking. "By
obeying each thought frankly," he maintained, "by harping, or, if you

will, pounding on each string, we learn at last its power. By the same obedience to other thoughts we learn theirs, and then comes some reasonable hope of harmonizing them" (*Works*, VI, 4). Or, more broadly, as he remarked later, "I might suggest that he who contents himself with dotting a fragmentary curve, recording only what facts he has observed, without attempting to arrange them within one outline, follows a system also,—a system as grand as any other, though he does not interfere with its vast curves by prematurely forcing them into a circle or ellipse . . . " (XII, 11-12). Emerson held, as an organicist will, that ultimately the relations between the apparently incompatible facts of experience were always there. Many of us are not capable of that belief, but if we are not, we can still respect Emerson's method, thus described, as a coherent and logical way of thinking, with characteristic virtues and uses, as well as limitations, like any other. It is not a closed system, but, as he says, it is a grand one, and it goes a long way, for me, toward explaining the larger consistency that most critics have sensed, without being able to account for it very well, in Emerson's work.

Weaknesses caused by the historical situation and by the inherent qualities of the doctrine can easily be forgiven; certain other weaknesses, which seem to be caused by Emerson's defective handling of the doctrine, must be counted as faults in his work. The most obvious of these probably lies in his cosmic optimism, which nearly all critics agree was often too easy. His statements were not always or even usually so carefully balanced and qualified as the one just cited. He tended to move too far toward the pole of unity and to ignore too much of our commonly frustrating and sometimes tragic experience of the confused, weltering world we live in. He knew about pain and poverty, love and hate, good and evil, accident and luck, and madness and ecstasy; but we sometimes feel, as he sometimes did, that he was not enough involved in them, that they did not have enough to do with his faith or his manner of arriving at it. We are too often asked to take his optimism straight, without the sense of its having been earned, and at such times we are likely to sympathize with objections made . . . to his enthusiastic, if not reckless, celebrations of the perfection of the universe. Cosmic optimism can be logically grounded on the premise that all things and events are ultimately organized in perfect unity, but it is a unity that we cannot see, and that Emerson cannot show us.

The fundamental tendency of the mind, according to him, and certainly it seems true of his mind, is to reduce all things to one law; and this tendency he felt to be right as well as inevitable. He was capable of saying, if not always of believing, that the "methodizing mind meets no resistance in its attempts." Moreover, he maintained, "It is necessary to suppose that every hose in Nature fits every hydrant; so only is combination, chemistry, vegetation, animation, intellection possible. Without identity at base, chaos must be forever" (*Works*, XII, 20). Faced with such a whole hog as that, a reader may well be excused for taking none. However, it is this belief which explains not only Emerson's optimism but all or nearly all of the difficult, paradoxical, daringly metaphorical, or at first glance apparently mystical passages in his works. It accounts for his feeling that every truth or partial truth, followed far enough, reaches identity with all other visions or versions of truth; that, if any man seems to disagree, "he only uses a different vocabulary from yours; it comes to the same thing" (*Journals*, II, 522) . . . It also supports his risky assertion in "Self-Reliance" that the farther we push our individual development, whatever direction it takes, the nearer we will come to comprehending the universal values. All these contentions are in some sense true, or at least reasonable, if we accept the assumptions that Emerson grounded on the organic metaphor; but most of us, having reservations about those premises, cannot wholly agree with his more extreme conclusions.

Another very frequent and cogent objection to Emerson's work is the pragmatic one that his essays and poems lack the organic unity that he aimed at in his thinking. F. O. Matthiessen, for example, says that "Emerson's writing was only too liable to exemplify the consequences of what he deemed the prevailing thought of his century, its reassertion of the Heraclitean doctrine of the Flowing" (p. 69 [in *American Renaissance*]). Matthiessen's objection is valid, if it can be grounded on the doctrine that the dynamism of romantic thought, properly understood, is not a flowing but a growing; not a featureless flux but the development of an organic structure with a strong though not rigid inner logic and an unbounded but not incoherent shape. Emerson's language, when he used the Heraclitean metaphor, as he did continually, betrayed his insecure grasp of the significantly different metaphor of the living plant. And his writings generally betrayed his insufficient appreciation of the fact that in an organic work of art there is just as great need for a tightly knit complex of inner functional relations as there is in a classical work for what we more familiarly know as form.

Most of the critics who have tried to defend Emerson against this objection have had to make so many concessions and reservations, and their comments have amounted to such faint praise, that the defense has fallen rather flat. . . . These observations indicate, rightly enough I think, that Emerson created very few individual works which can be said to have anything like the organic unity which the New Critics and their predecessors in the romantic tradition have taught us to expect. Nevertheless I believe that Emerson was a great writer, and therefore that something remains to be explained.

The most promising approach that I have seen to such an explanation was first suggested by [W. T.] Harris in an article published in 1884, in which he expanded and specified his previous discussion of unity in Emerson's work, using terms more nearly in harmony with his own predilection for the Hegelian system. Besides the Coleridgean organic unity which he had previously discussed, and which he now limited to works of "literary art" (that is, poems), he discovered in Emerson's prose essays a "dialectic unity" which was "an unfolding of the subject according to its natural growth in experience."[5] The words "unfolding" and "growth" make this look like a kind of unity that might be considered both logical and organic, which I am inclined to think it is. Harris went on to show in detail how Emerson had arrived at this unity in the essay "Experience," and to make a very good case for his successful practice of a dialectic method in his composition generally. Blair and Faust, adopting Harris' hint, have suggested [in "Emerson's Literary Method"] a dialectic quality in Emerson's structural use of the "twice bisected line" of Plato, to whom Emerson himself ascribed a dialectic method in philosophy. . . .

It seems to me that the twice bisected line, which implies a fourfold hierarchy of values corresponding to "conjecture, faith, understanding, reason" (*Works*, IV, 69), marks the course of a blind alley, and that Emerson explains his own method, if not Plato's, better when he abandons that rather stiff and geometric analogy and says that Plato "represents the privilege of the intellect, the power, namely, of carrying up every fact to successive platforms and so disclosing in every fact a germ of expansion," adding that such "expansions are organic" (IV, 81-82). With that reservation, I should like to see Harris' method of analysis applied still more widely to Emerson's work.

As Emerson indicated in "The American Scholar," his usual practice was to take the scattered facts of experience and try to establish relations among them, without any forcing or rearrangement. Sometimes he went about it, limiting himself more or less closely to one point of view, by beginning with the crudest considerations he could think of and working up to the highest and rarest abstractions of the organic idea. In *Nature*, for example, he started from "Commodity" and went through "Beauty," "Language," and "Discipline" to arrive at "Idealism," "Spirit," and "Prospects." Similarly, in *The Conduct of Life,* he began with "Fate," "Power," and "Wealth," proceeded by a somewhat wandering course through "Culture," "Behavior," "Worship," and "Considerations by the Way," and reached his climax in "Beauty" and "Illusions." At other times he attempted a larger scope by moving back and forth, or up and down, from statements of diversity to declarations of unity and back again to diversity. The first series of *Essays* might be so arranged, roughly, if we were to classify "History" and "Self-Reliance" under the heading of diversity; "Compensation" and "Spiritual Laws" under unity; "Love," "Friendship," "Prudence," and "Heroism" under practical experience, or diversity again; and "The Over-Soul," "Circles," "Intellect," and "Art" under ideal integration, or unity. A complete analysis would of course reveal many further complexities in the structure of the book, but some such main lines as these would probably persist.

It must be admitted, as a defect, that in some individual essays Emerson seems to have begun by assuming the final unity as his premise and forcing it on the facts of experience in such a way as to do them violence; for example, in "Compensation" or "Circles." But these were not published as separate works by Emerson, and to discuss them without some correcting reference to "History" or "Prudence" in the same series is to misrepresent his range of thought.

The real difficulty in the first *Essays*, and in most of Emerson's work, is to find a middle between the extremes. His own simile of the dotted curve is appropriate; there are gaps, perhaps in his thinking, certainly in his writing, left unfilled. Melville's simile in *Moby Dick*, that the chapters of a book grow as the branches and twigs of a tree from its trunk, is more in harmony with what Emerson was driving at. It seems to me, in fact, that not only Melville but other novelists such as Henry James, who was careful to let his stories grow from the smallest possible germs of thought, or Faulkner, whose Yoknapatawpha chronicles appear to have developed from an almost invisible seed in *Soldier's Pay* to the marvellous jungle of his later works, have practiced Emerson's method more consistently, and to better effect, than he was able to do himself. He was at his best, I feel, in such a work as "Experience," where he admitted most liberally the confused and contradictory character of human life and refrained from building on it any further in the direction of unity than the nature of his materials permitted.

Emerson's feeling, however, was somewhat different from mine, and his application of the organic theory was made from another point of view. He believed, as he explained in *Nature,* that "The standard of beauty is the entire circuit of natural forms,—the totalit *t* of nature. . . . Nothing is quite beautiful alone; nothing but is beautiful in the whole" (I, 23-24). Or, as he said with even more emphasis in "Each and All," beauty for him was an attribute of the whole universe and could not exist or be satisfactorily embodied, any more than truth could, in any separate fragment. Every true perception of beauty therefore depended on the whole context, the universe, in which every object had its one proper place, and out of which it could not be seen without distortion and ugliness. Any attempt to create a separately complete representation of either beauty or truth would be an almost sacrilegious wrenching at the universal fabric. Emerson's works, then, may be said to have been intended as glimpses of this and that aspect of the macrocosm in its whole vastness, however imperfectly seen, rather than as microcosmically complete and perfect organisms in themselves. For that reason, if for no other, the individual works are likely to lack the very qualities of structural relatedness, wholeness, and unity which Emerson considered the most important attributes of the universal reality.

Emerson's defects, then, when they are not the defects of his time and of the inherent nature of his ideas, may fairly be called the defects of his qualities; and, when all is said, they are minor. If we look at the whole body of his work from as near as we can come to his own point of view, remembering that he always aimed at the universal rather than at any particular unity, and that the relation between his various statements is usually organic in the progressive, or dialectic, rather than in any static sense, we can see that his philosophy and his art have a consistency which need not be referred to his character but which inheres fundamentally in the organic metaphor and which is often most present in the tension and dynamic balance of his most contradictory pronouncements. Historically, though he was by no means our greatest literary artist, he was perhaps the most important thinker and writer we have had, the first to make our declaration of cultural independence effective, and the chief pioneer of romanticism (that is to say, of modern thought and art) in this country. . . .

From "Emerson and the Organic Metaphor," *PMLA*, 69 (March 1954), 117-30.

1. *Science and the Modern World* (New York, 1925), pp. 104, 112.

2. Pepper, *The Basis of Criticism in the Arts* (Cambridge, Mass., 1945), p. 74. My discussion of the differences between organicism, formism, and mechanism is based largely on Pepper's *World Hypotheses* (Berkeley, 1948).

3. *The Complete Works of Ralph Waldo Emerson,* ed. Edward Waldo Emerson (Boston, 1903-04), 12 vols.

4. For a full discussion of organicism and its root metaphor, see Pepper, *World Hypotheses,* pp. 280-314.

5. "The Dialectic Unity in Emerson's Prose," *Jour. of Speculative Philos.,* XVIII (April 1884), 195. (This paper was first delivered as a lecture at the Concord School of Philosophy in the summer of 1882.)

NEWTON ARVIN

The House of Pain: Emerson and the Tragic Sense

IT IS not true that Emerson's optimism is quite so unmodulated as it has often been represented as being, or that he was so incapable as Yeats thought him to be of the Vision of Evil. I have been speaking of Evil just now in the sense of suffering and frustration, but even if it is a question of moral evil, of human malignancy, depravity, and vice, it is not true that Emerson averted his gaze from it quite so steadily as his detractors have said. Neither suffering nor wickedness is his primary theme; they are not even secondary; in his work as a whole they are tiny patches of grayness or blackness in a composition that is flooded with light and high color. But, even if we ignore the sermons of his youth, in which the New England sense of guilt and sinfulness sometimes throbs and shoots as painfully as it ever does in Hawthorne—even if we ignore these early writings, it is not true that Emerson's view of human nature was a merely smiling and sanguine one. To be sure, it was the feebleness of men, their incompetence, their imbecility, that he castigated, when he was in this vein, more often than their depravity. But, when he chose, he could express himself as unsentimentally as any moral realist on the brutishness of which men are capable. It was no mere idealist who said, with some humor indeed, in speaking of the Norman Conquest: "Twenty thousand thieves landed at Hastings."

This bluntness is very characteristic of him, and when he was really deeply stirred by the spectacle of systematic cruelty and injustice, as he was during the long anguish of the anti-slavery struggle, he could wrench off certain specious masks and disguises as unsparingly, as realistically, as any of his Calvinist ancestors could have done. Read the "Address" he delivered at Concord on the anniversary of the emancipation of slaves in the West Indies if you wish to have a glimpse of Emerson the moral realist. They tell us, he says in his speech, that the slave-holder does not wish to own slaves for the love of owning them, but only because of the material advantages his ownership brings. Experience, however, he goes on to say, does not bear out this comfortable evasion, but shows "the existence, beside the covetousness, of a bitterer element, the love of power, the voluptuousness of holding a human being in his absolute control." Men are capable, says Emerson, of liking to inflict pain, and the slave-holder "has contracted in his indolent and luxurious climate the need of excitement by irritating and tormenting his slave."

It is hard to see how the Vision of Evil, at least for a moment, could be much keener or more terrible than this; and in the whole slavery connection Emerson said a good many things almost equally piercing. But it remains true that his animadversions on human wickedness, like his allusions to human suffering, are closer to the circumference than to the center of Emerson's thought; they give his writings their moral chiaroscuro, but they are not dominant, and I have perhaps dwelt too long on them. His controlling mode of thought, even in his later and more skeptical years, is a certain form of Optimism and *not* a form of the Tragic Sense, and what I should like to say now is that, however we may ourselves feel about this philosophy, it was one that rested not only on a deep personal experience but on a considered theory of Evil, and moreover that this was a theory by no means peculiar to Emerson, or original with him: on the contrary, it had a long and august tradition behind it in Western thought and analogies with the thought not only of Europe but of the East. To put it very briefly, it is the theory that identifies Evil with non-existence, with negation, with the absence of positive Being. In his own writings Emerson expressed this doctrine first in the famous "Address" at the Divinity School at Harvard in 1838, the manifesto of his heterodoxy. "Good is positive," he said to the graduating class that day. "Evil is merely privative, not absolute: it is like cold, which is the privation of heat. All evil is so much death or nonentity. Benevolence is absolute and real."

Such language as this has become terribly unfamiliar to us, and Heaven knows for what good reasons, in our own guilt-ridden and anxious time; some of us may find it hard to believe that reasonable men ever entertained such a view. The truth is, however, that it is not only a philosophical but an essentially religious view, and that its sources, to speak only of the West, are in the Platonic and Neo-Platonic tradition and in Christian theology on the side on which it derives from that tradition. It was from these sources, indeed, that Emerson drew his theoretical Optimism. When Plato identified the Good with absolute reality, and Evil with the imperfectly real or the unreal, he was speaking a language beyond Tragedy; and let us not forget that he proposed to banish tragic poetry from his ideal Republic—to banish it on the ground that the wise and virtuous man will wish to control the emotions of grief and sorrow rather than to stimulate them. As for Plotinus, the greatest of the Neo-Platonists, whom Emerson read with such excitement in the few years before the "Address" at the Divinity School, he too denied that Evil can have a part in real existence, since this—real existence—is by definition good. "If then evil exists," says Plotinus, "there remains for it the sphere of not-being, and it is, as it were, a certain form of not-being." The sentence reads very much like Emerson's own.

At any rate it was this Neo-Platonic denial of any absolute or ultimate reality to Evil that seems to have found its way into Christian orthodoxy in the writings of St. Augustine—"a man," as Emerson says, "of as clear a sight as almost any other." The Manicheans had attributed to Evil a positive and independent existence, and Augustine as a young man had fallen under their spell; but he had broken away from them at the time of his conversion, and steeped as he was in the thought of the Neo-Platonists, he arrived at a theory of Evil that, on one level, seems indistinguishable from theirs. "Evil has no positive nature," he says in *The City of God*; "but the loss of good has received the name 'evil.' " In itself it is purely negative, a diminishment or corruption of the good, for, as he says, "no nature at all is evil, and this is a name for nothing but the want of good." Of course, as one need not say, Augustine does not deny that *sin* has a kind of reality, but he conceives of it as an essentially negative reality—as a rejection or refusal of the Good, not as an ultimate and independent essence in itself.

No sane man, of course, whatever his metaphysics, can refuse to recognize that wrong-doing is in some sense a *fact*; and Emerson was much too clear-sighted a moralist not to find a place in his thought, as Augustine had done, for what his ancestors had called "sin," though his account of it is not quite the same as Augustine's. He accounts for it, in a more purely transcendental way, by distinguishing between what is real to the intellect and what is real to the conscience—real, that is, in the conduct of life itself. "Sin, seen from the thought," he says, "is a diminution, or *less*; seen from the conscience or will, it is pravity or *bad*. The intellect names it shade, absence of light, and no essence. The conscience must feel it as essence, essential evil. This it is not; it has an objective existence, but no subjective." Objectively, that is, and when the conscience speaks, the savagery of the slave-holder is real enough; subjectively, and when the voice of the mind is heard, that savagery is seen for the "absence of light," the essential unreality, it is. Despite their differences, Augustine and Emerson are saying at least not dissimilar things.

Convictions such as this, at any rate, are at the heart and core of his philosophic optimism. Both sin and suffering, moral and natural evil, *appear* in experience; but they are indeed appearances, not ultimate realities; what reality they have is relative, external, transitory; absolutely speaking, they are shadows, phenomena, illusions. We may, in our time, find such convictions as these mistaken, but let us recognize them for what they are. They are convictions of an essentially religious sort, and like Plato's, or Plotinus's, or Augustine's, they are in themselves inconsistent with the Tragic Sense. We are in the habit of assuming that the most serious and profound apprehension of reality is the Sense of Tragedy; but it may be that, in assuming this, we ourselves are mistaken. It may be that there are points of view from which the Tragic Sense must be seen as serious and profound indeed, but limited and imperfectly philosophical. It may even be that there can exist a kind of complacency of pessimism, as there is certainly a complacency of optimism; and that many of us in this age are guilty of it. We hug our negations, our doubts, our disbeliefs, to our chests, as if our moral and intellectual dignity depended on them. And indeed it does—so far as the alternative is to remain *this side* of Tragedy, and to shut our ears and eyes to the horrors of experience. Our impatience with Emerson is by no means wholly baseless. We feel, and we have a right to feel, that, if we take his work as a whole, there is a certain distortion in the way it reflects the real world; a certain imbalance and deformation in the way in which the lights and shadows are distributed. The shadows are too meager, and sometimes they are too easily conjured away. We have a right to feel that, too much of the time, Emerson is speaking with a lightheartedness that seems to keep him on this side of Tragedy.

What I have been trying to suggest, however, is that we cannot justly leave him there—that the time has come to remind ourselves that it is possible to reach beyond Tragedy, as well as to remain on the hither side of it; that this is what the religious sense has always done; that Tragedy, as a poetic form, has flourished only rarely, in periods of disbelief and denial; and that, for Emerson, disbelief and denial were simply impossible, ultimately, in the light of his transcendental faith. We may well dislike the tone he often takes, but if we wait patiently enough, we shall find him taking other tones; and in the end we must recognize that, whatever our own convictions are, the best of Emerson is on the other side of Tragedy. I have tried to show that he did not simply *find* himself there; if he had got beyond Tragedy, it was because he had *moved* beyond it. "It requires moral courage to grieve," says Kierkegaard; "it requires religious courage to rejoice." We would be less than just, I think, if we denied that Emerson's courage was both moral and religious.

His acquaintance with the religious literature of the world was very wide; it was by no means confined to the Christian or even the Western tradition; and perhaps we might concede that his perspective was wider and deeper than that which most of us can command. While he was still in his thirties he began to read some of the Hindu scriptures as they appeared in translation; and he quickly recognized in them philosophical and religious insights that seemed at times to be mere anticipations of his own. When he read the Upanishads, or the *Bhagavad-Gita*, or the *Vishnu Purana*, what he found in them was a conception of the ultimate and impersonal Ground of Being—of Brahma—that had much in common with the Absolute of the Neo-Platonists and with his own God or Over-Soul. He found more than that. He had already arrived at the conviction that, as he said, "Within and Above are synonyms"; that the Over-Soul and the individual soul are one; that the kingdom of God, as the gospel says, is within you. The Upanishads only confirmed him in this conviction—confirmed him by their expression of the doctrine that the Absolute Self and the individual self are identical; that Brahma and Atman, as they say, are one; that, as they also say, *"That* art *Thou."* This too was a doctrine that left the Tragic Sense behind it. According to the Upanishads, the man who, as a result of intense discipline and concentrated meditation, attains to a knowledge of the Self—call it either Brahma or Atman, for they are the same—has transcended the illusory realm of human wretchedness and wickedness, and is beyond either. "He who knows the Self," says the *Brihadaranyaka Upanishad,* "is honored of all men and attains to blessedness. He who meditates upon Brahma as such lacks nothing and is forever happy. He who meditates upon Brahma as such becomes himself invincible and unconquerable. . . . Indeed, the Self, in his true nature, is free from craving, free from evil, free from fear."

When one reads passages like this, and there are many of them, one finds it easy to understand why the literary form of Tragedy—the tragic drama—is unknown in Sanskrit literature. In any case, I do not wish to imply that there are no important differences, even in this connection, among the thinkers I have spoken of; that the Neo-Platonist Plotinus, the orthodox Christian Augustine, and the authors of the Upanishads were perfectly at one in their view of Good and Evil; and that Emerson is indistinguishable from any of them. The differences are vital, some of them, and certainly there is much in Emerson, especially in his tone, that would have struck his great predecessors as very dubious indeed. I have intended only to suggest that it is superficial to rule out the whole of him, once for all, on the ground that he lacked the Vision of Evil; to see him as nothing but a transcendental American optimist of the midnineteenth century; to fail to see that his view of these things was in a great philosophic and religious tradition; and that he rejected Tragedy not because he was by temperament wholly incapable of tragic insight but because it seemed to him that, as Karl Jaspers has said, "tragedy is not absolute but belongs in the foreground"; it belongs, as he says, "in the world of sense and time," but not in the realm of transcendence. It belongs, let us say, in the world of appearance, of the relative, of illusion; not in the realm of transcendent reality and truth in which Emerson's faith was complete. . . .

From "The House of Pain: Emerson and the Tragic Sense," *The Hudson Review,* 12 (Spring 1959), 37-53.

SELECTED BIBLIOGRAPHY

Works

Editions

The Complete Works of Ralph Waldo Emerson. The Centenary Edition. Ed. Edward Waldo Emerson. 12 vols. Boston: Houghton, Mifflin, 1903-04; rpt. New York: AMS PRess, 1968. The standard edition.

The Early Lectures of Ralph Waldo Emerson. Ed. Stephen E. Whicher et al. 2 vols. Cambridge, Mass.: Harvard Univ. Press, 1959 and 1964.

The Journals and Miscellaneous Notebooks of Ralph Waldo Emerson. Ed. William H. Gilman et al. 8 vols. to date. Cambridge, Mass.: Harvard Univ. Press, 1960-70. This edition is superseding the Emerson-Forbes edition of the journals.

The Journals of Ralph Waldo Emerson. Ed. Edward Waldo Emerson and Waldo Emerson Forbes. 10 vols. Boston: Houghton Mifflin, 1909-14. Formerly the standard edition.

Young Emerson Speaks: Unpublished Discourses on Many Subjects. Ed. Arthur C. McGiffert, Jr. Boston: Houghton Mifflin, 1938; rpt. Port Washington, N.Y.: Kennikat Press, 1968. A selection of Emerson's early sermons.

Selections

Useful and inexpensive selections include those edited by Brooks Atkinson (*Selected Writings.* New York: Modern Library, 1950); Reginald L. Cook (*Selected Prose and Poetry.* Rinehart Edition. New York: Holt, Rinehart & Winston, 1950); Mark Van Doren (*The Portable Emerson.* New York: Viking, 1957); Stephen E. Whicher (*Selections from Ralph Waldo Emerson.* Riverside Edition. Boston: Houghton Mifflin, 1957).

Letters

The Correspondence of Emerson and Carlyle. Ed. Joseph Slater. New York: Columbia Univ. Press, 1964. A new edition of the 1883 collection.

The Letters of Ralph Waldo Emerson. Ed. Ralph L. Rusk. 6 vols. New York: Columbia Univ. Press, 1939. The standard but not all-inclusive edition.

Biography and Criticism

Alcott, Amos Bronson. *Ralph Waldo Emerson: An Estimate of His Character and Genius, in Prose and Verse.* Boston: A. Williams, 1882; rpt. New York: Haskell House, 1968.

Anderson, John Q. *The Liberating Gods: Emerson on Poets and Poetry.* Coral Gables, Fla.: Univ. of Miami Press, 1970.

Beach, Joseph Warren. *The Concept of Nature in Nineteenth-Century English Poetry.* New York: Macmillan, 1936; rpt. New York: Russell & Russell, 1966.

Berry, Edmund Grindlay. *Emerson's Plutarch.* Cambridge, Mass.: Harvard Univ. Press, 1961.

Bishop, Jonathan. *Emerson on the Soul.* Cambridge, Mass.: Harvard Univ. Press, 1964.

Braswell, William. "Melville as a Critic of Emerson." *American Literature*, 9 (November 1937), 317-34.

Brooks, Van Wyck. *The Life of Emerson*. New York: E. P. Dutton, 1932.

Brown, Percy W. "Emerson's Philosophy of Aesthetics." *The Journal of Aesthetics & Art Criticism*, 15 (March 1957), 350-54.

Brown, Stuart Gerry. "Emerson's Platonism." *The New England Quarterly*, 18 (September 1945), 325-45.

Cabot, James Elliot. *A Memoir of Ralph Waldo Emerson*. 2 vols. Boston: Houghton, Mifflin, 1887; rpt. New York: AMS Press, 1969.

Cameron, Kenneth W. *Ralph Waldo Emerson's Readings*. Raleigh, N.C.: The Thistle Press, 1941; rpt. New York: Haskell House, 1969.

Caponigri, A. Robert. "Brownson and Emerson: Nature and History." *The New England Quarterly*, 18 (September 1945), 368-90.

Carpenter, Frederic Ives. *Emerson Handbook*. New York: Hendricks House, 1953; new ed. 1967.

Cowen, Michael H. *City of the West: Emerson, America, and Urban Metaphor*. New Haven, Conn.: Yale Univ. Press, 1967.

Dewey, John. *Characters and Events: Popular Essays in Social and Political Philosophy*. Vol. I. New York: Henry Holt, 1929; rpt. New York: Octagon Books, 1970.

Emerson, Edward W. *Emerson in Concord: A Memoir*. Boston: Houghton Mifflin, 1889; rpt. New York: Garrett Press, 1970.

Feidelson, Charles, Jr. *Symbolism and American Literature*. Chicago: Univ. of Chicago Press, 1953.

Gray, Henry D. *Emerson: A Statement of New England Transcendentalism as Expressed in the Philosophy of Its Chief Exponent*. Stanford Univ., Calif.: The University, 1917; rpt. New York: Frederick Ungar, 1958.

Hoeltje, Hubert H. *Sheltering Tree*. Durham, N.C.: Duke Univ. Press, 1943; rpt. Port Washington, N.Y.: Kennikat Press, 1965.

Hopkins, Vivian C. *Spires of Form: A Study of Emerson's Aesthetic Theory*. Cambridge, Mass.: Harvard Univ. Press, 1951; rpt. New York: Russell & Russell, 1965.

Hubbell, George S., ed. *A Concordance to the Poems of Ralph Waldo Emerson*. New York: H. W. Wilson, 1932; rpt. New York: Russell & Russell, 1967.

Lauter, Paul. "Truth and Nature: Emerson's Use of Two Complex Words." *ELH*, 27 (March 1960), 66-85.

Lewis, R. W. B. *The American Adam: Innocence, Tragedy, and Tradition in the Nineteenth Century*. Chicago: Univ. of Chicago Press, 1955.

Miles, Josephine. *Ralph Waldo Emerson*. Minneapolis: Univ. of Minnesota Press, 1964.

Nicoloff, Philip L. *Emerson on Race and History: An Examination of English Traits*. New York: Columbia Univ. Press, 1961.

Paul, Sherman. *Emerson's Angle of Vision: Man and Nature in American Experience*. Cambridge, Mass.: Harvard Univ. Press, 1952.

Perry, Bliss. *Emerson Today*. Princeton, N.J.: Princeton Univ. Press, 1931; rpt. Hamden, Conn.: Shoe String Press, 1969.

Porte, Joel. *Emerson and Thoreau: Transcendentalists in Conflict*. Middletown, Conn.: Wesleyan Univ. Press, 1966.

Reaver, J. Russell. *Emerson as Mythmaker*. Gainesville: Univ. of Florida Press, 1954.

Rusk, Ralph L. *The Life of Ralph Waldo Emerson*. New York: Scribner's, 1949; rpt. New York: Columbia Univ. Press, 1957.

Whicher, Stephen E. *Freedom and Fate: An Inner Life of Ralph Waldo Emerson*. Philadelphia: Univ. of Pennsylvania Press, 1953; 2nd ed., 1969.

Young, Charles Lowell. *Emerson's Montaigne*. New York: Macmillan, 1941.